SCHUBERT

SYMPHONY IN B MINOR ("Unfinished")

An Authoritative Score

Schubert's Sketches · Commentary

Essays in History and Analysis

NORTON CRITICAL SCORES

BACH **CANTATA NO. 4**
edited by Gerhard Herz

BACH **CANTATA NO. 140**
edited by Gerhard Herz

BEETHOVEN **SYMPHONY NO. 5 IN C MINOR**
edited by Elliot Forbes

BERLIOZ **FANTASTIC SYMPHONY**
edited by Edward T. Cone

BRAHMS **VARIATIONS ON A THEME OF HAYDN, OPP. 56A AND 56B**
edited by Donald M. McCorkle

CHOPIN **PRELUDES, OPUS 28**
edited by Thomas Higgins

DEBUSSY **PRELUDE TO "THE AFTERNOON OF A FAUN"**
edited by William W. Austin

HAYDN **SYMPHONY NO. 103 IN E-FLAT MAJOR ("DRUM ROLL")**
edited by Karl Geiringer

MOZART **PIANO CONCERTO IN C MAJOR, K. 503**
edited by Joseph Kerman

MOZART **SYMPHONY IN G MINOR, K. 550**
edited by Nathan Broder

PALESTRINA **POPE MARCELLUS MASS**
edited by Lewis Lockwood

SCHUBERT **SYMPHONY IN B MINOR ("UNFINISHED")**
edited by Martin Chusid

SCHUMANN **DICHTERLIEBE**
edited by Arthur Komar

STRAVINSKY **PETRUSHKA**
edited by Charles Hamm

Franz Schubert

SYMPHONY IN B MINOR
("Unfinished")

An Authoritative Score
Schubert's Sketches · Commentary
Essays in History and Analysis

REVISED

Edited by

MARTIN CHUSID
NEW YORK UNIVERSITY

W · W · NORTON & COMPANY · INC · *New York*

Contents

PREFACE TO THE REVISED EDITION

One of the regularly recurring musical phenomena of the nineteenth and twentieth centuries has been the uncovering of Schubert manuscripts, as if death could diminish but not halt the composer's renowned creativity. In fact, the process of discovery has accelerated in recent years as a result of the intensive search for all possible sources by the editors of the *Neue Schubert-Ausgabe* (New Schubert Complete Edition). One such discovery, a group of manuscripts at the archive of the Wiener Männergesang-Verein, contained a completely unknown fragment of the Scherzo for the *Unfinished,* and this suggested a revision of the Norton Critical Score. Excerpts from Christa Landon's important article *New Schubert Finds* have been included to describe the manuscript, and to provide necessary historical information.

The newly discovered fragment, mm. 10–20 of the orchestral score for the Scherzo, is printed below (pp. 68–69), and the opportunity of a second edition has been taken to re-edit portions of the music, to bring the bibliography up to date, and to make other necessary changes and corrections. Most of the alterations in the score of the completed movements result from a re-evaluation of the dynamic marking ⟩ . Additional experience editing Schubert has now convinced me that more of these signs are accents rather than short decrescendo markings. Schubert had a tendency to enlarge the accents as the dynamic level increased, or as he hastily covered large stretches of music paper. It may be noted that an interpretation increasing the number of accents and decreasing the decrescendo markings results in a more precisely articulated, somewhat less ponderous performance. The resultant sonorous ideal, I believe, is far more suitable to the musical style of the early decades of the nineteenth century than the organ-like ebb and flow appropriate for much orchestral music later in the century. I would like to thank Mrs. Landon for generously sharing her materials, and *The Music Review* for allowing us to reprint portions of her article.

MARTIN CHUSID

February 1971

PREFACE TO THE FIRST EDITION

The editor's purpose has been to present an accurate edition of the orchestral score and the piano sketches of the *Unfinished,* together with pertinent historical data, critical commentary, and some possible answers to important questions about the work that have arisen during the past hundred years.

The analytical notes have been written with the full awareness that a great work of art invites analysis from many points of view and that the principal benefits of analysis ultimately remain with the analyst. These notes, therefore, are intended to supplement rather than replace individual study. Stress has been laid on matters of general style as reflected in other works by Schubert as well as the *Unfinished.* Since analytical terminology tends to change from time to time and even from place to place, an attempt has been made to discuss those musical aspects that might have interested or reflected the point of view of Schubert's contemporaries (e.g., Carl Czerny or E. T. A. Hoffmann). It is expected that the individual musician or student will examine the symphony with reference to his own training and interests.

I would like to thank my colleague Martin Bernstein for his careful reading of large sections of the editor's commentary and for his many helpful suggestions. He is, of course, not responsible for errors of fact or assumption. I owe an even greater debt to my wife, Anita, who helped in ways too numerous to mention.

MARTIN CHUSID

THE
HISTORICAL BACKGROUND

The Historical Background

For the past century Schubert's Symphony No. 8 in B minor (D. 759), known as the *Unfinished,* has proved to be his most popular and best-loved work. It has long been one of the most frequently performed works in the entire orchestral repertory and, in recent years, has also become one of the most frequently recorded. At the same time, the symphony has had an unusual history. It was not performed until thirty-seven years after Schubert's death, and there is a minimum of information concerning the circumstances of its composition. The signed manuscript is dated 1822, six years before the composer's death, yet not a single known document refers to the work in unequivocal fashion until 1842, some twenty years later.

As a result it has been possible—indeed, almost fashionable—to ask more questions concerning the work than can be answered satisfactorily. For what individual, organization, or event was the symphony originally intended? The intrinsic value of the work was recognized by the two men who were in possession of the manuscript and they compared it with symphonies of Beethoven. Why, then, was it not made available for performance or publication until 1865? And—in view of the undisputed excellence of the two completed movements—why did Schubert leave the symphony uncompleted?

The autograph manuscript of the orchestral score has a title page bearing Schubert's signature, the place of composition (Vienna), and the date October 30, 1822.[1] At some time, probably during its composer's lifetime,

---

1. See the line reproduction of the title page in *The Schubert Reader,* a documentary biography compiled by Otto Erich Deutsch, New York, 1947, p. 256. This indispensable tool will be referred to hereafter as *SR.* A companion volume by Deutsch entitled *Schubert: Memoirs by his Friends,* New York, 1958, will be referred to as *S:MF.* —The house in which Schubert was living at the time he wrote the *Unfinished* still stands in the oldest portion of Vienna, the inner city.

this manuscript passed into the hands of Josef Hüttenbrenner and subsequently was brought to the home of Josef's brother Anselm, near Graz. Here it remained until 1865. Schubert also wrote piano sketches for the symphony, of which the first pages (more than half of the first movement) have been lost.[2] The sketches never left Vienna and were unknown to the Hüttenbrenner family. Neither the manuscript nor the piano sketches bear a dedication, although the Hüttenbrenners claimed that Schubert had intended both the dedication and the orchestral score of the symphony for Anselm.

In September of 1823, Schubert had received an honorary diploma from the Styrian Musical Society at Graz, dated April 6 of the same year. Anselm was a member and later an official of the organization, and apparently by virtue of his friendship with Schubert had received the honorary document to pass on to the young composer. Anselm then gave the diploma to Josef, who delivered it to Schubert. In Josef's words "Schubert gave it [the manuscript of the *Unfinished*] to me for Anselm, as thanks for having sent him, through me, the Diploma of Honour of the Graz Musical Society."[3] About 1868 Josef altered this account somewhat and now stated that "Schubert gave it to me out of gratitude for the Diploma of Honour from the Graz Music Society, and dedicated it to the *Society* and Anselm; I brought the diploma to Schubert."[4]

At this point it seems appropriate to review Schubert's relationship with the Hüttenbrenner family. Anselm (1794–1868) had come to Vienna in 1815 from the vicinity of Graz in the Austrian province of Styria. During his first year in the city, he met Schubert as a fellow student of composition at the home of Antonio Salieri (1750–1825), the well-known composer of operas who had studied with Gluck, had been Mozart's successful rival at the Viennese court, had taught Beethoven— principally lessons in the setting of Italian texts to music—and in his last years was even to teach the young Liszt. Schubert had been Salieri's student since 1812.

2. Since there are no piano sketches remaining for the completed symphonies (i.e. the first six and the "Great" C major) or for the Symphonic Sketch in E of 1821, it has been assumed—probably rightly so—that Schubert attached special significance to the B minor work.

3. *S:MF*, p. 430. Excerpt from a letter addressed by Josef Hüttenbrenner to Johann Herbeck and dated March 8, 1860. See also footnote 22. In a letter to his brother Andreas, dated Feb. 11, 1867, Josef specifically says "Schubert gave me the Symphony, outside the Schottentor, for the Graz Diploma of Honour, and dedicated it to Anselm." *S:MF*, p. 442.

4. *S:MF*, p. 193; my italics.

By 1817, Anselm and Schubert were good friends and that same year Schubert wrote a set of variations for piano (D. 573) on a theme from Anselm's first string quartet, Op. 3. During these early years Schubert and Anselm also sang together in a male vocal quartet.[5] In the fall of 1818, Anselm returned to Graz for a year, and on his marriage in 1821 resettled there permanently. He and Schubert remained friendly for the rest of the latter's short life. Several warm letters from Schubert to Anselm are still extant.[6] Anselm visited Vienna often; on these occasions the two musicians were seen together at public performances and social gatherings. While on a trip to Graz in the summer of 1827 Schubert visited Anselm's home several times.

Anselm, who was a good pianist, took part in performances of Schubert's music both in Vienna and Graz, and wrote waltzes based on Schubert's song *Der Erlkönig* that were published in 1821, the same year as the song itself. As mentioned above, he was particularly active in the affairs of the Styrian Music Society, a group that performed works by Schubert as well as awarding him the honorary diploma in 1823. Anselm's Requiem Mass in C minor was played at the memorial services for Schubert held at St. Augustine's church on December 23, 1828, and shortly thereafter he wrote a composition entitled *Memorial for Schubert in Mournful Voices at the Piano*.[7] The evidence indicates that Schubert was fond of Anselm and respected him as a musician. But Schubert's relations with his brother, Josef, were less consistently cordial.

Josef Hüttenbrenner (1796–1882) was an amateur singer (tenor), pianist, and composer who in 1815 or 1816 had heard of Schubert from Anselm. According to Josef, Schubert had begun to send him songs— *Minona* and *Rastlose Liebe* in 1816, *Der Kampf* in 1817, and a copy of *Die Forelle* in 1818. On a visit to Vienna during the summer of 1817, Josef met Schubert, and in December of 1818 he settled permanently in the capital city as an official in the Austrian Ministry of the Interior. Josef cultivated the young composer's friendship assiduously, and during 1820 even lived at the same house with him.

Josef's interest in Schubert, however, was not completely altruistic.

---

5. *SR*, p. 63.

6. *SR*, Nos. 124, 142, 149, 1007.

7. Anselm's memoirs of Schubert and other documents are collected in *S:MF*. Much additional information was lost when Anselm burned his diary in 1841. In a letter dated April 4, 1842, he wrote "I had kept it [the diary] for about 20 years and *Schubert* certainly appeared in it several hundred times between the years 1815 and 1828." *S:MF*, p. 402.

On May 19, 1819, Schubert wrote a letter from Vienna addressed to Anselm and gave it to Josef for transmission to Graz. On the back of Schubert's letter Josef appended a note to a third brother, Heinrich (1799–1830), who was something of a poet.[8] Included were the following remarks:

> . . . For the present, make it your business to write an opera libretto for Schubert—and tell Schröckinger the same.—There is a fee to be had at the same time.—Your names will be known all over Europe.—Schubert will actually shine as a new Orion in the musical heavens. . . . Write soon about your decision concerning Schubert.—Fare you well.
>
> Your
> Josef.[9]

Josef, then, recognized Schubert's genius, but also saw potential monetary rewards and an opportunity to bask in reflected glory. It was not many years after the letter was written that Josef was entrusted by Schubert to conduct the composer's business affairs (from 1821 to 1823).[10] At one point Josef even took charge of putting Schubert's manuscripts in order. During this period of service, Josef acquired several manuscripts for himself, including the operas *Des Teufels Lustschloss* and *Claudine von Villa Bella*.[11]

The most significant biography of Schubert to appear in the 19th century was that of Heinrich Kreissle von Hellborn. It first appeared in Vienna late in 1864, although the official date of publication was 1865. Both Josef and Anselm were alive at that time and had contributed material to the biography. Other friends of Schubert were also consulted, and the following remarks were included; they were never contradicted, either by Josef or Anselm.

> For Anselm he [Schubert] had a true and sincere regard associated with the interest which he bestowed upon the musical efforts of his friend. Josef, on the contrary, as he grew in the course of time more intimate with the musician, became an ardent Schubert worshipper, and showed himself so zealous an admirer, that Schubert was far more anxious to keep away

8. Schubert apparently never met Heinrich but set two of his verses to music, a song, *Der Jüngling auf dem Hügel* (D. 702), and a quartet for male voices, *Wehmut* (D. 825, No. 1).

9. *SR*, p. 119.

10. See the numerous entries in the *SR* for those years, including several accounts of monetary transactions (*SR*, Nos. 339 and 348).

11. The latter opera is based on a text by Goethe. Unfortunately, during the winter of 1848 servants used the second and third acts of the manuscript to help light a fire at Josef's lodgings in Vienna. As a result, only the overture and first act remain.

from him than to encourage him; and he would regret his too fulsome adulation with words of irony—'Why that man likes everything I do.'

At this point Kreissle appends a footnote including the following:

> A gentleman, intimate with Schubert and [Josef] Hüttenbrenner, described to me (perhaps a little overcolouring the picture) the relations existing between these two men, in a manner that tempts one to believe that they only loved at a distance. This is the passage:—'Josef, who would take no denial in his worship and zeal for Schubert, became almost an object of aversion to the musician; he often put him off rudely, and treated him so harshly, that we nicknamed Schubert "The Tyrant"—of course, good temperedly.' [12]

After 1823 Schubert and Josef were no longer as close as they had been previously. In striking contrast with the numerous documents of the preceding years, there are no remaining communications between the two men from 1824 to Schubert's death in 1828. It is reasonable to assume, therefore, that Josef acquired the manuscript of the *Unfinished* some time between the date of composition and the end of 1823, possibly a short while after he had delivered the honorary diploma.

Schubert's letter of thanks to the Styrian group for the diploma is dated September 20, 1823, and contains the following promise: "In order to give musical expression to my sincere gratitude as well, I shall take the liberty before long of presenting your honourable Society with one of my symphonies in full score." [13]

Did Schubert begin the Symphony in B minor for the Graz Society? On the surface this would not seem to be likely, since Schubert's composition is dated some five months earlier than the diploma. However, the proposal for Schubert's membership provides a possible clue to the sequence of events. It is dated April 10—that is, four days *after* the date of the diploma itself (April 6). Therefore, if the date of the proposal is correct, it was in all probability only a formality for the records of the organization. But, in that case, when was Schubert first suggested for membership? The idea may well have originated before the end of October 1822. If so, then Schubert probably began the work for the Styrian Society. Several items of evidence support this possibility. In addition to the Hüttenbrenner family, the secretary of the society, Johann Baptist Jenger (1792–1856), was also friendly with Schubert. Jenger, another

12. From Heinrich Kreissle von Hellborn, *The Life of Franz Schubert*, transl. by Arthur D. Coleridge, London, 1869, I, 129–30.
13. *SR*, pp. 289–90. Interestingly enough, in view of a hypothesis to be discussed later (see p. 98), Beethoven had been elected an honorary member of the society in 1821—a fact that Schubert must have known.

enthusiastic amateur musician, had lived in Vienna in 1818 and at that time came to know and admire Schubert.

Furthermore, newspaper notices and reviews indicate that Schubert's music was being performed in Graz during the fall of 1822 with considerable success. On September 14, 1822, for example, the *Grazer Zeitung* reported that "Schubert's vocal quartet, 'The Little Village,' made a great sensation, here as in the capital. It had to be sung more than once. A wholly perfect, thoroughly original composition, it cannot fail to be speedily accepted everywhere." [14]

It seems logical to assume that the proposal for the honorary membership would originate at the time these performances were causing a public "sensation." Schubert's influential friends in the society could, while advancing such plans, informally acquaint the composer of their intentions, if only to ascertain his reaction to the projected honor.

If this line of reasoning is close to the truth, then a dedication to the society would certainly be in order, and must have been Schubert's intention. However, he could not dedicate an uncompleted work. We are left then with the most intriguing, the most puzzling of all the questions: why did he not complete the symphony?

The evidence—empty pages of score following the orchestral fragment of the third movement, and the partial state of completion of this same movement in the piano sketches—indicates that Schubert was interrupted in the course of composition. The interruption could have been the result of internal (i.e. compositional) problems, as is suggested later in this study, or it may have been externally caused (i.e. illness, pressure to provide other works, personal problems, etc.) . However, if Schubert felt *both* the desire and the need to produce such a work after the interruption, and if the problems were purely external, then he should have returned to the composition once these obstacles were removed. Here the critical words are "desire and need after the interruption." In fact, both desire and need can be demonstrated—and in the very next years, 1823 and 1824.

In addition to the Styrian group, the Linz Musical Society awarded Schubert an honorary degree during the same year, 1823.[15] Furthermore,

14. *SR*, p. 233. Three concerts in Graz included works by Schubert during September and October of 1822; see *SR*, pp. 233f. and 236. At this time there were also performances of his music in Linz and Vienna.

15. *SR*, p. 288. Deutsch also suggests that it was in 1823 that Schubert formally declined a request for an orchestral work by a "Herr von Bäutel" (perhaps Josef Peitl, a former teacher of Schubert's) . An undated letter, *SR*, pp. 264–65, indicates that he had earlier acceded to von Bäutel's request. The letter is cited on p. 99 of this study.

a letter of early 1824 indicates how passionately the young composer was concerned with the idea of writing symphonies.[16] With an intense personal interest and opportunities for performance, there would seem to have been every possible reason for him to have completed a work with such promising beginnings. But he did not, and an entire literature of conjecture has arisen as a result.[17]

There is one aspect that apparently has not been emphasized by writers on the subject. This concerns Schubert's feelings of uncertainty with regard to composing instrumental music during the years 1818 to 1822. From the time he completed his Sixth Symphony (D. 589, October 1817–February 1818) to the date of the *Wanderer Fantasy* (D. 760, November 1822), Schubert left approximately twice as many fragments of compositions as he did completed, larger instrumental works. Moreover, these fragments are not completed compositions, or movements, with portions that had been lost, as are many of Schubert's earlier fragments (e.g. the String Quartets in B♭, D. 68, and C minor, D. 103). In point of fact, at no other time in his career did Schubert fail to complete so many compositions, and the fragments include at least three, possibly four, symphonies.[18]

There is compelling reason to believe that Schubert's uncertainty at this time resulted from a confrontation with Beethoven's instrumental music. Earlier, while he was a student of Salieri, his feelings toward Beethoven were mixed—witness the critical entry from his diary of June 16, 1816.[19] In 1817, however, he ceased his formal studies with Salieri

16. The letter is partially cited on p. 99 below.

17. For a survey of the more serious suggestions see the portions reprinted below from Otto Erich Deutsch's article, *The Riddle of Schubert's Unfinished Symphony*. A new hypothesis by the editor is contained below in the essay entitled *Beethoven and the Unfinished*.

18. Among the symphonies, in addition to the *Unfinished*, are piano sketches for seven movements of a Symphony in D (D. 615, May 1818), the Symphonic Sketch in E (D. 729, August 1821), and sketches for a larger instrumental work found together with the sketches for the opera *Die Zauberharfe* (D. 644, 1819–20); see Fritz Racek, *Von den Schubert-Handschriften der Stadtbibliothek* (*Wiener Schriften, IV*), Vienna, 1956. The other fragments are D. 613, D. 618A, D. 625, D. 655, D. 703 (*Quartettsatz*), and possibly D. 346–49, D. 994, D. 601, and D. 605.

19. "It must be beautiful and refreshing for an artist [i.e. Salieri] to see all his pupils gathered about him, each one striving to give of his best for his jubilee, and to hear in all these compositions the expression of pure nature, free from all the eccentricity that is common among most composers nowadays, and is due almost wholly to one of our greatest German artists [i.e. Beethoven]; that eccentricity which joins and confuses the tragic with the comic, the agreeable with the repulsive, heroism with howlings and the holiest with harlequinades, without distinction, so as to goad people to madness instead of dissolving them in love, to incite them to laughter instead of lifting them up to God. To see this eccentricity banished from the circle of his pupils

and, at least in the instrumental realm, turned towards Beethoven's compositions. Hans Koeltzsch, who published an extensive investigation of Schubert's piano music in 1927, has pointed to numerous relationships between Beethoven's sonatas and those by Schubert written at this time. Later in this book, additional evidence will be cited indicating Beethoven's influence on Schubert's generalized conception of the symphony, as well as evidence of Beethoven's influence on the *Unfinished* itself. At this point one further fact may be mentioned. During April of 1822, the same year he wrote the *Unfinished*, Schubert's *Eight Variations on a French Song*, for piano duet, were published. Aside from some dances this was his first instrumental work in print. It is inscribed:

> Dedicated to Herr Ludwig van Beethoven
> By his devoted worshipper and admirer.

The earliest unequivocal reference to the *Unfinished* dates from April 4, 1842, some twenty years after the work was composed. A letter from Anselm Hüttenbrenner to his brother Josef written on that date includes the information that "The unfinished symphony in B minor is marked: Vienna, 30 October 1822." [20] The information was apparently intended for a proposed catalogue of Schubert's music being prepared at that time by Aloys Fuchs. In 1853 Anselm arranged the two completed movements of the *Unfinished* for piano, four hands.

The next mention of the work dates from about 1858 and comes from Josef. Compiling notes for Ferdinand Luib, one of the most assiduous of the would-be Schubert biographers of the time, he wrote: "To Anselm Schubert also dedicated a symphony in B minor, which, however, is not completed; it can hold its own with any of Beethoven's." [21]

On March 8, 1860, Josef wrote to Johann Herbeck, chorus master of the Vienna Männergesangverein and artistic director of the Gesellschaft der Musikfreunde. Herbeck, a composer as well as conductor and one of the most influential Viennese musicians of his day, was an ardent advocate of Schubert's music. Josef sought to interest Herbeck in, among other things, his brother Anselm's music. After some rather intemperate claims as to its value, he offers as bait the *Unfinished:* Anselm "possesses a treasure . . . in Schubert's *'B minor Symphony,'* which we *place on*

---

and instead to look upon pure, holy nature, must be the greatest pleasure for an artist who, guided by such a one as Gluck, learned to know nature and to uphold it in spite of the unnatural conditions of our age." *SR*, p. 64.

20. *S:MF*, p. 402.

21. *S:MF*, p. 76.

a level with the great C major Symphony, his instrumental swan song, and with *any of Beethoven's.*" [22] Herbeck took the bait five years later.

The first printed reference to the *Unfinished* dates from 1863 and occurs in the autobiographical article written by Anselm for Wurzbach's *Biographisches Lexikon des Kaisertums Oesterreich.* This was followed in 1865 by a reference in Kreissle's biography of Schubert. Kreissle openly urged Anselm no longer to withhold the work from the public.[23]

Later that year Johann Herbeck went to Graz and obtained the manuscript from Anselm by promising to perform the work together with a composition by Anselm. He actually did so at a concert of the Gesellschaft der Musikfreunde on December 17 of the same year. The woodwinds were doubled, and the finale of Schubert's Third Symphony in D major was added as the first of many attempts to complete the work.

Herbeck never returned the orchestral manuscript to Anselm. Instead, he allowed it to be printed by Spina, Vienna, 1866. Later he gave the manuscript to Nikolaus Dumba, an indefatigable collector of Schubert autographs who had already acquired the piano sketches. Dumba, in turn, bequeathed both orchestral version and piano sketches in 1900 to the same Gesellschaft der Musikfreunde, their present owners.

The first performance was a success. On November 4, 1866, Herbeck conducted the two completed movements alone. On December 13 of the same year, there was a performance in the Leipzig Gewandhaus, conducted by Karl Reinecke, who arranged the work for piano solo (Spina, Vienna, 1867). Performances followed in England (1867) and Graz (1871), and the work has remained a favorite ever since. For the Graz performance the Styrian Musical Society printed programs claiming the dedication for itself, perhaps on the basis of Josef Hüttenbrenner's conflicting statements on the subject.[24] With this insufficiently substantiated program announcement by the Graz Society, the *Unfinished* was launched on its future course: well-appreciated performances combined with poorly documented conjectures concerning its origin and history.

22. *S:MF*, p. 430. The original is complete in Ludwig Herbeck's biography of his father, *Johann Herbeck, Ein Lebensbild,* Vienna, 1885, pp. 164–65.

23. *Op. cit.*, p. 292.

24. See Deutsch, *The Riddle of Schubert's Unfinished Symphony,* in *The Music Review,* I (1940), 47 (not included in the portions reprinted below, p. 91 f.); L. Herbeck, *op. cit.*, p. 165; and p. 4 above.

THE SCORE
OF THE SYMPHONY

*including the Piano Sketches
and the Scherzo Fragment*

INSTRUMENTATION

2 Flutes
2 Oboes
2 Clarinets in A
2 Bassoons

2 Horns: in D in 1st and 3rd mvts., in E in 2nd mvt.
2 Trumpets in E
3 Trombones
Timpani

Violin I
Violin II
Viola
Violoncello
Double Bass

SYMPHONY IN B MINOR

I

* See timpani signature of the Scherzo fragment, p. 68.

pp
pp
20
fz
p
fz
p
fz
fz
[p]
pp
fz
[p]
pp
arco
pizz.
fz
p
arco
pizz.
fz
p
arco
pizz.
fz
p

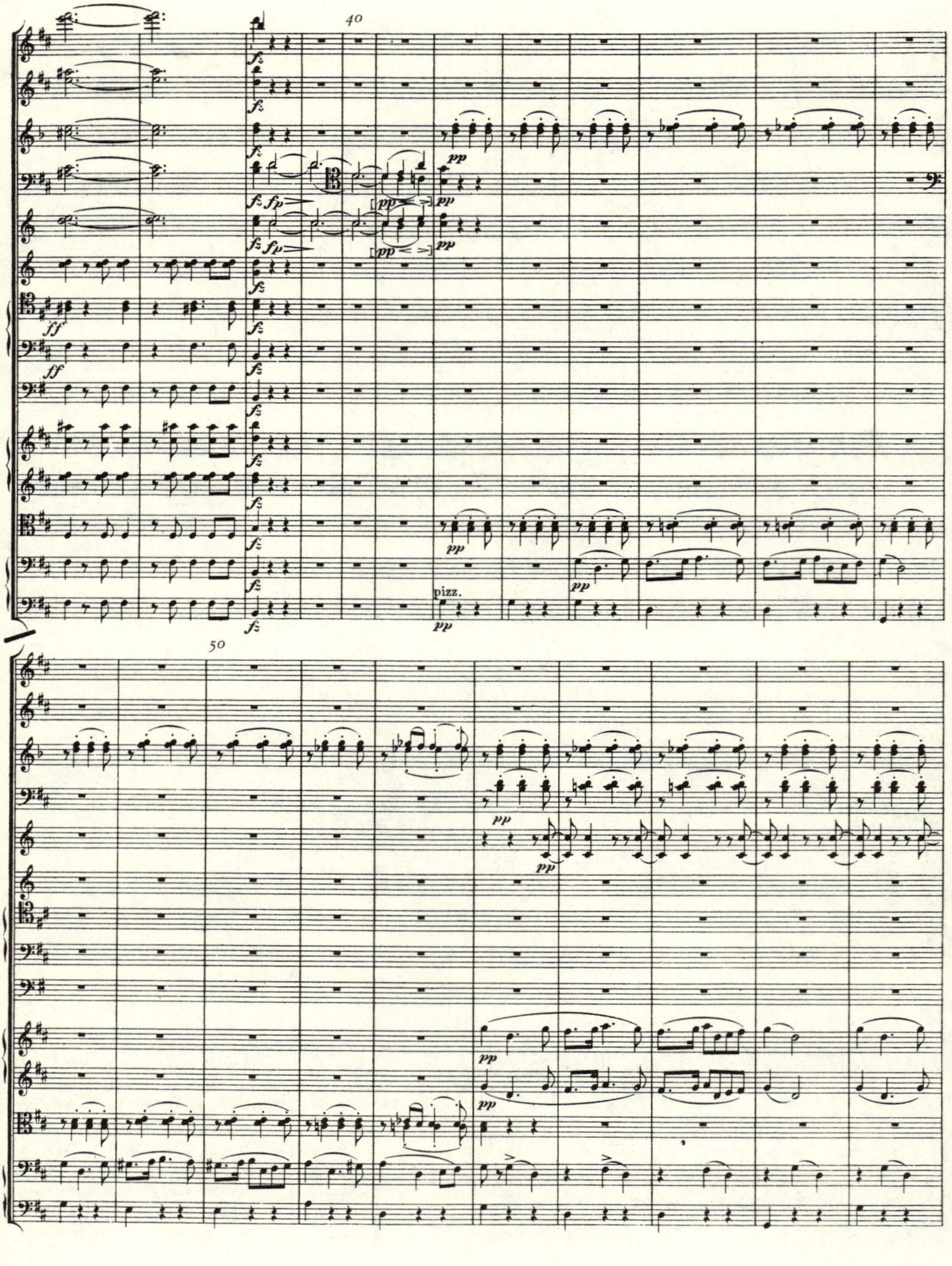
40
ff
fz
fp
pp
pizz.
50

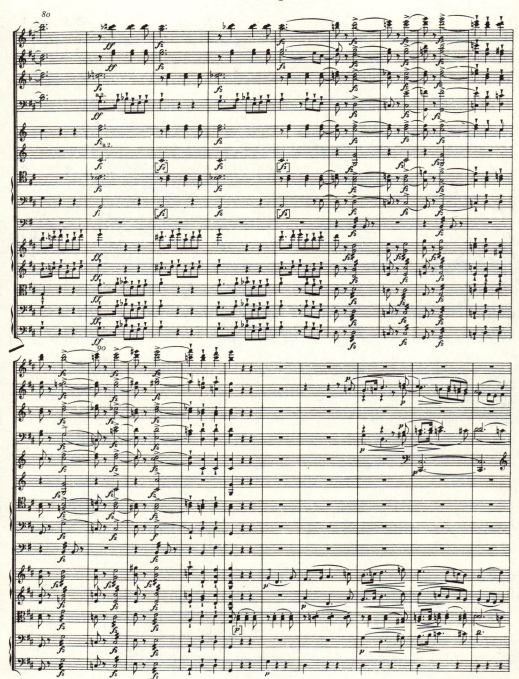

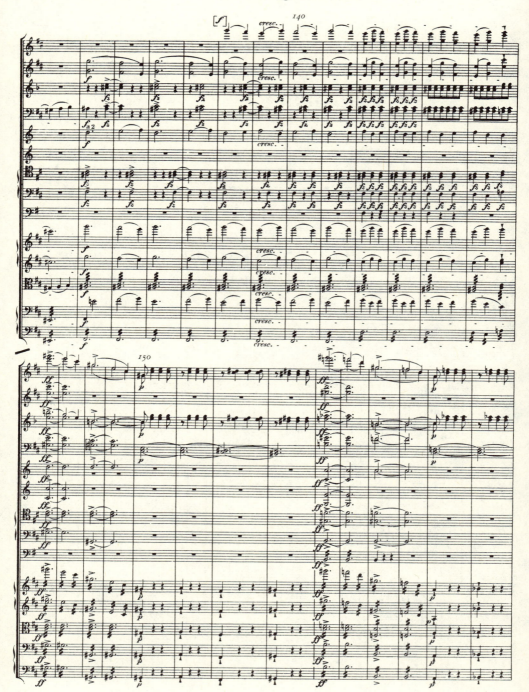

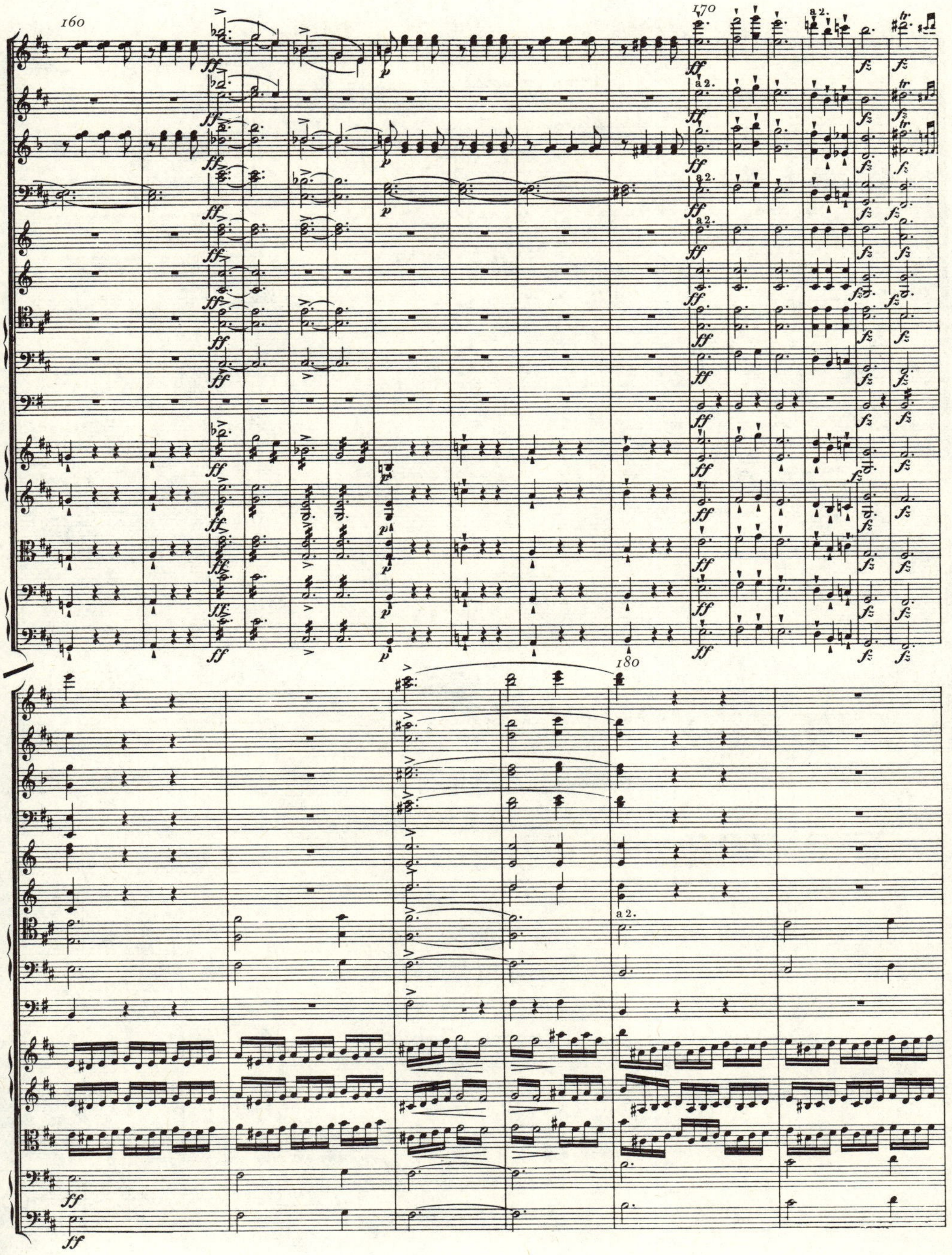
160
170
180
a 2.
ff
p
fz
tr

I: Allegro moderato

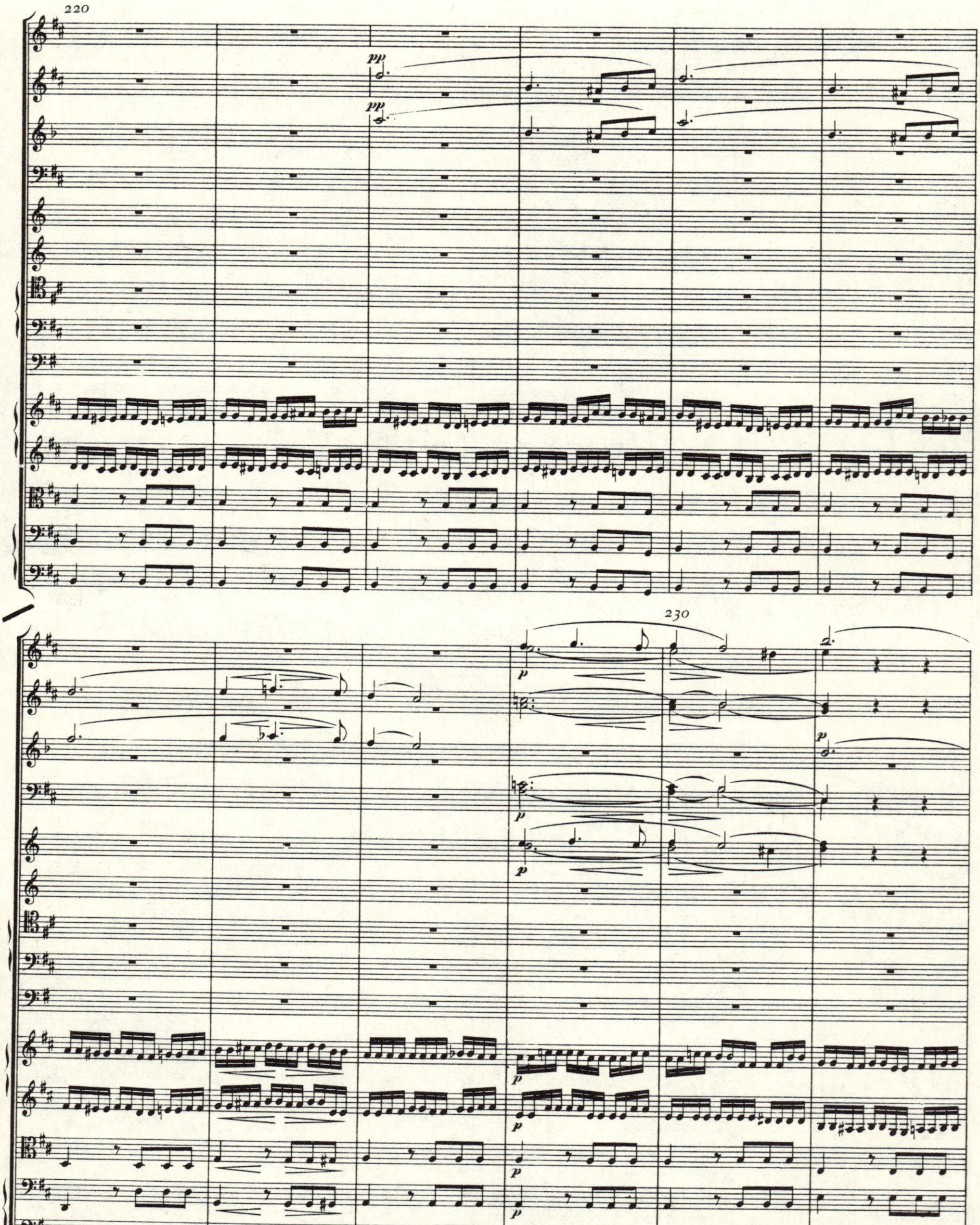
220
pp
pp
230
p
p
p
p
p
p
p
p

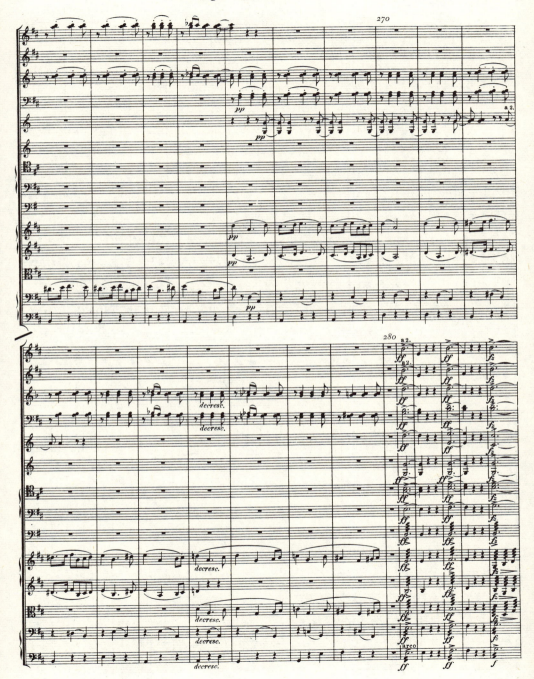

I: Allegro moderato

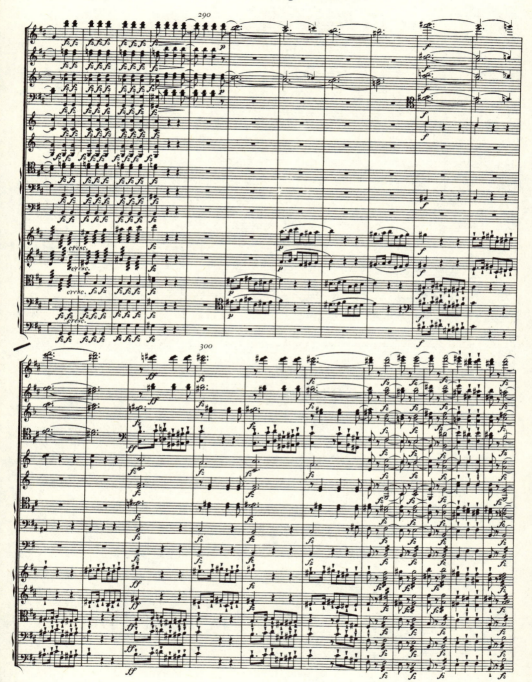

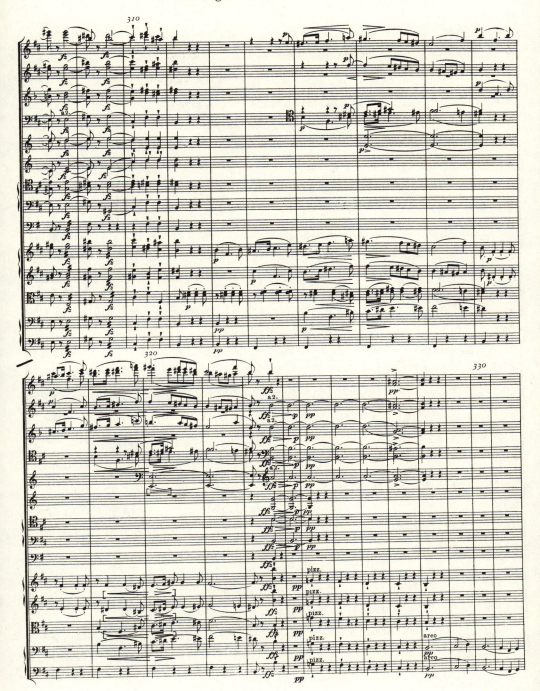

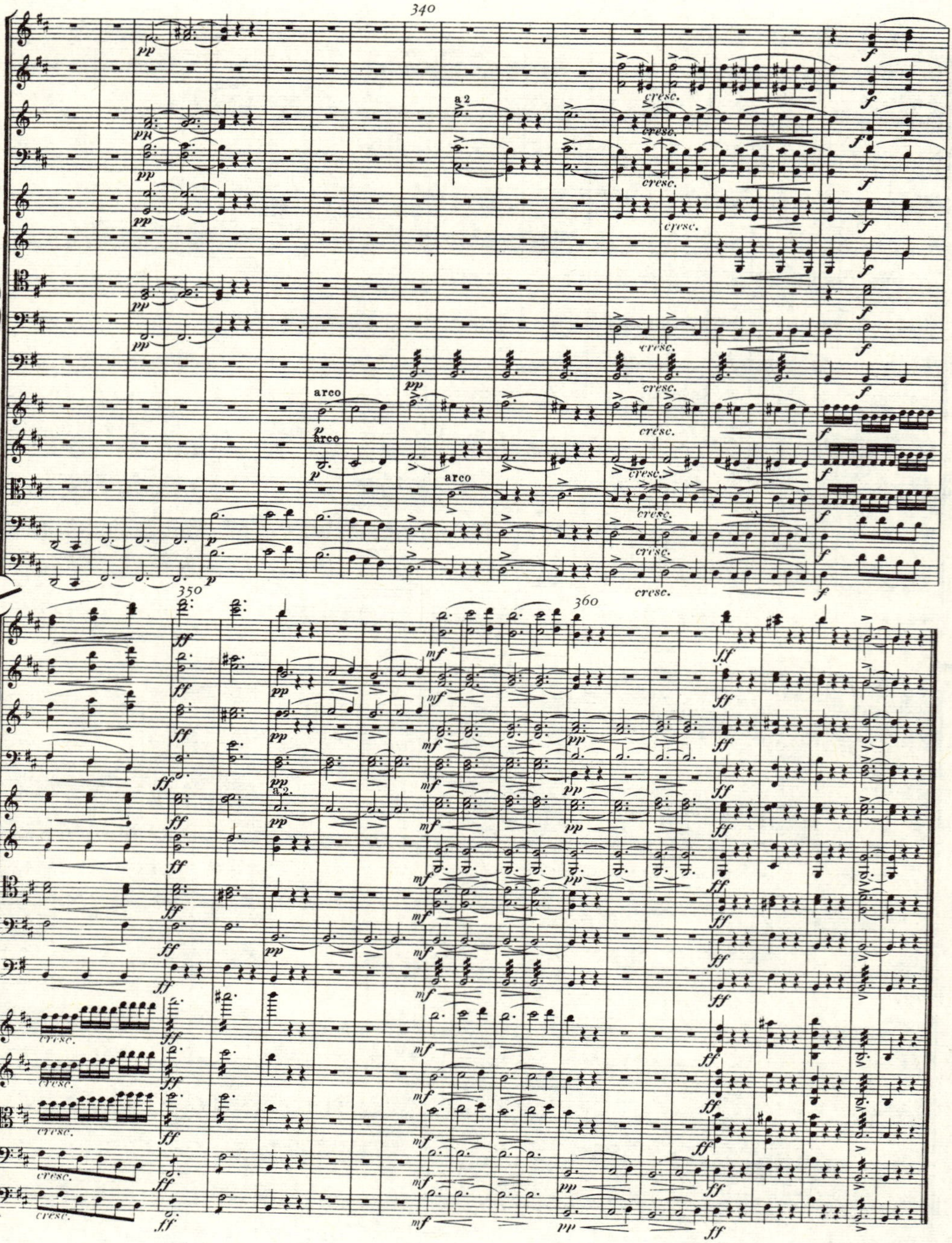
340
a 2
arco
arco
arco
pp
p
cresc.
f
350
360
ff
mf
pp
a 2.

II

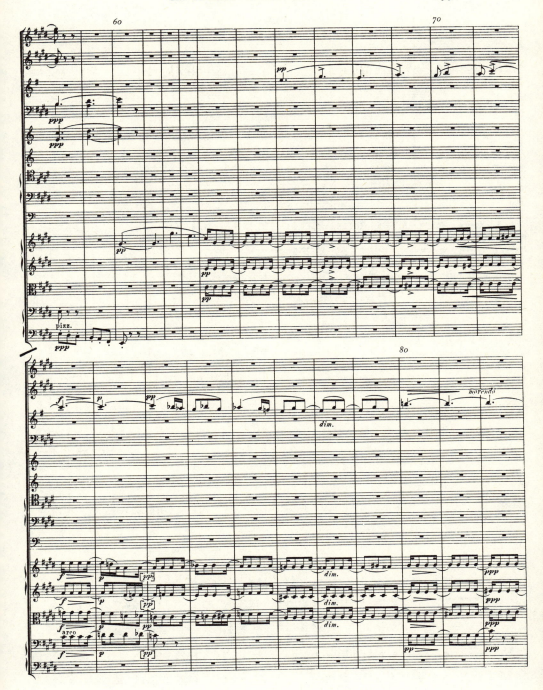

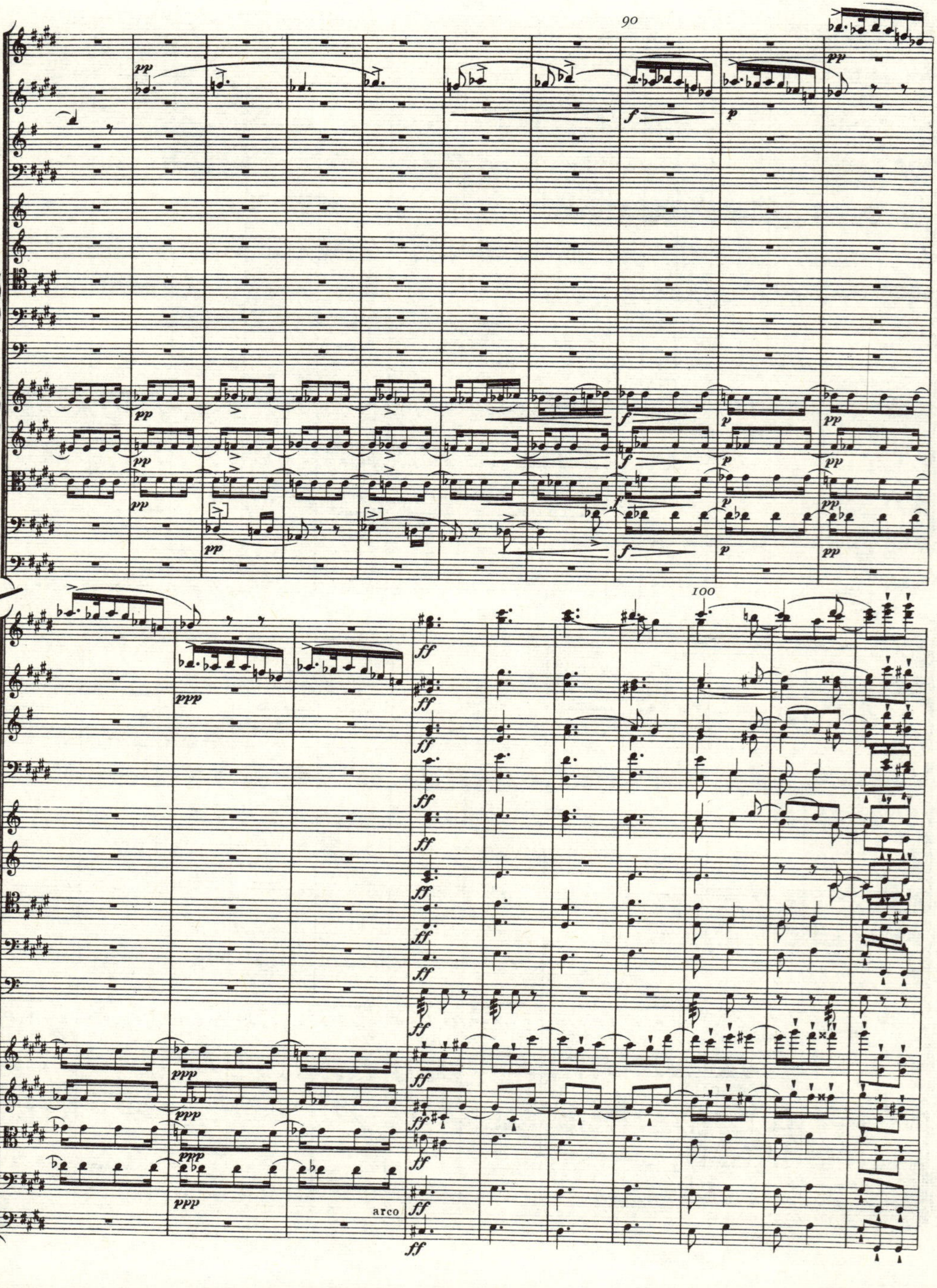
90
100
arco

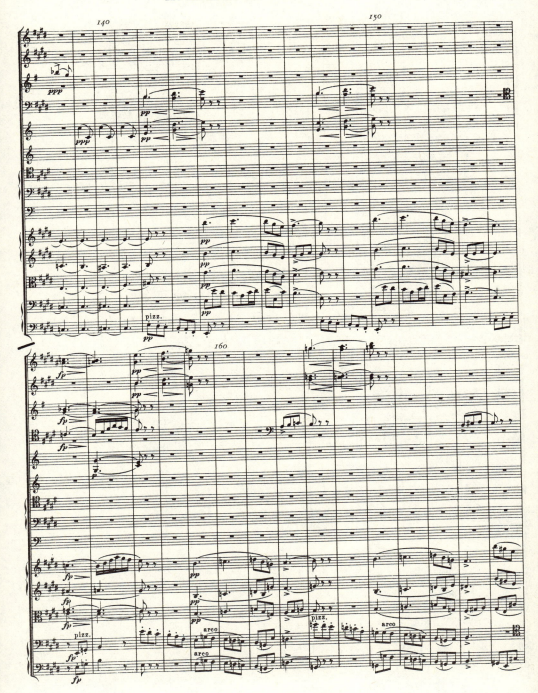

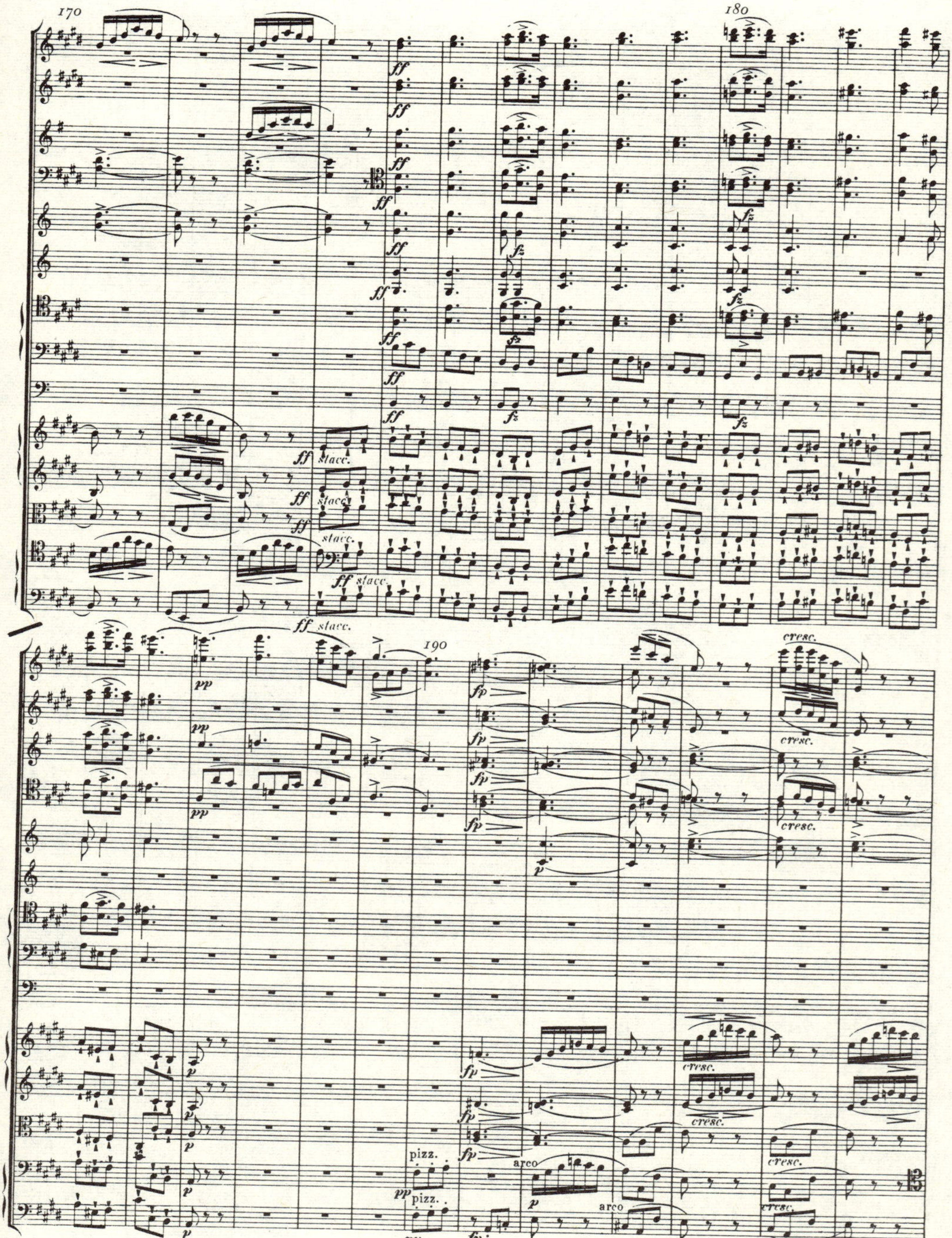
170
180
190
ff
stacc.
fz
pp
fp
p
cresc.
pizz.
arco

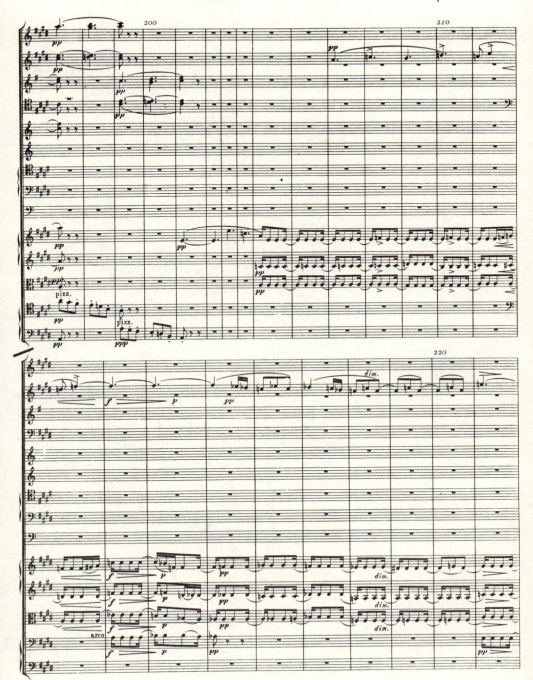

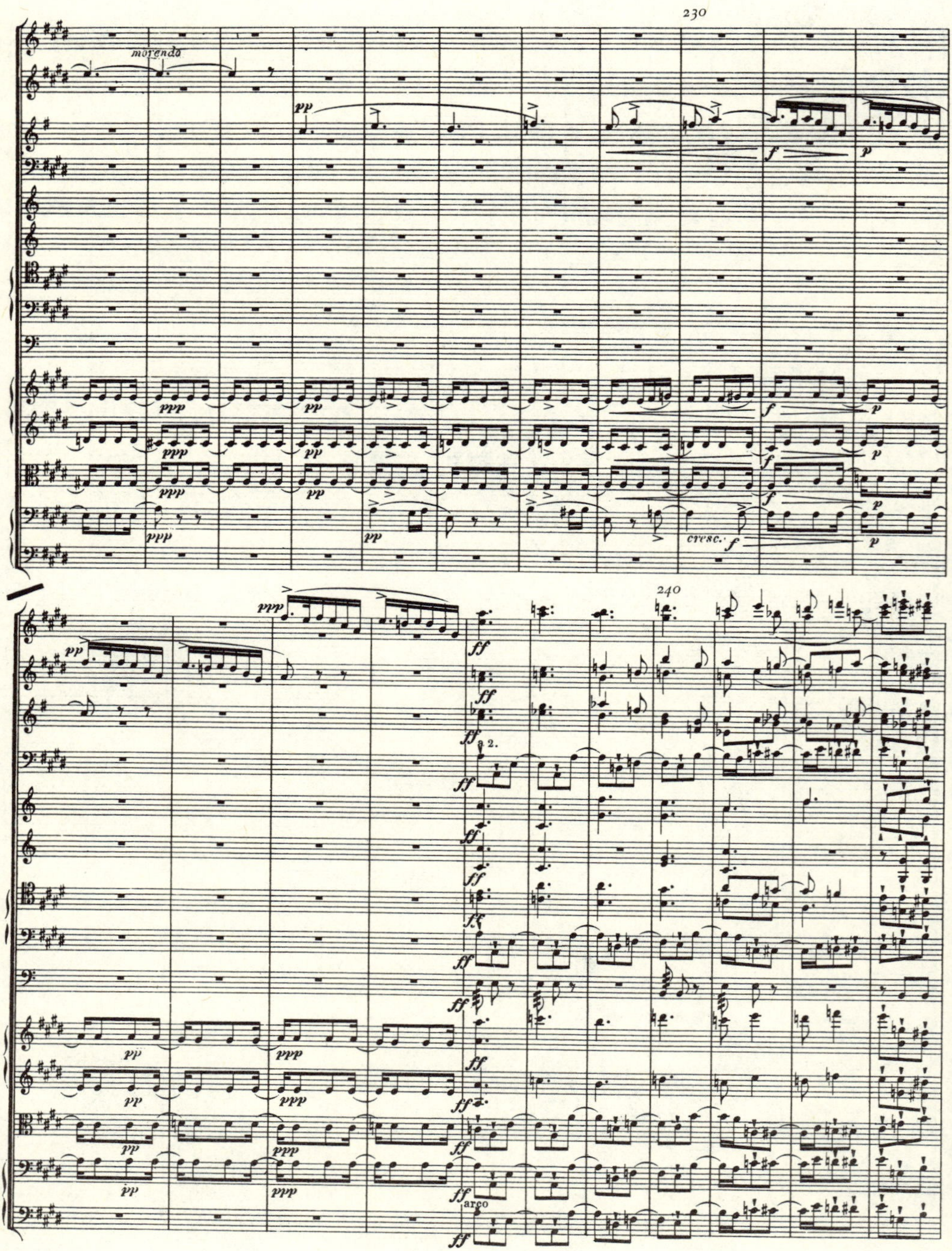
230
morendo
pp
f
p
ppp
cresc.
240
ff
a 2.
arco

Textual Note

The basis for this edition is the Schubert *Gesamtausgabe* (Complete Edition), Leipzig, 1882–97. The symphonies were edited by Johannes Brahms, with editorial notes by Eusebius Mandyczewski.[1] Emendations have been made with reference to the facsimile of the manuscript published by Drei-Masken-Verlag, Munich, 1924; the more important of these are listed below.

Surprising as it may seem, the present edition is the first to print all the extant portions of the piano sketches together with the score in one and the same volume. Previously the sketches were to be found only in manuscript form, as part of the facsimile edition, or separated from the printed score, in the volume of editorial comments to the *Gesamtausgabe*.[2]

In general, the manuscript of the score is remarkably clean with no major corrections, although there are important differences between the fragmentary piano sketch of the first movement[3] and the final version: compare especially the transition to the second theme, the continuation of the second theme, and the coda.

Unlike Beethoven in his later symphonies (i.e. the Seventh, Eighth, and Ninth), Schubert does not adopt the modern grouping of instruments in his manuscript. Instead he follows one of the most common 18th-century arrangements, with the violins and violas at the top of the score page and the cellos and double basses at the bottom. The woodwinds are found immediately below the violas, followed by brass and percussion. Again as in

1. Eusebius Mandyczewski (1857–1929) was the chief editor for the Schubert Complete Edition. Entirely responsible for editing the songs, church music, and male part-songs, he collaborated with others on the majority of the chamber works, the four-hand piano music, and the compositions for female and mixed chorus. He also wrote most of the editorial notes. Mandyczewski was well known in Vienna as a teacher and conductor, held the position of archivist for the Gesellschaft der Musikfreunde from 1887, and was a close friend and amanuensis for Johannes Brahms in the last years of the latter's life.

See the important discussion of Mandyczewski's activities by Maurice J. E. Brown, in his *Essays on Schubert*, New York, 1966, pp. 187–93.

2. Two publishers have reproduced the Scherzo portions of the piano sketches, as well as the first nine measures of the orchestral score, together with the completed movements. They are Philharmonia (edited by Otto Erich Deutsch and Karl Heinz Füssl, Vienna, 1959) and Eulenberg (London, 1961 and 1967). Eulenberg's Scherzo contribution is in facsimile. It should be noted, however, that neither publisher included the extant sketches for the other movements.

3. Only 93 measures of the piano sketches for the first movement—portions of the recapitulation and the coda—survive.

many 18th-century scores, the trumpets and timpani are grouped together below the horns. The trombones, in the 18th century usually found only in opera orchestras,[4] are placed between the timpani and the cellos.

Schubert's manuscript of the *Unfinished* is troublesome to read only in the area of dynamic markings. For example, it is almost impossible to distinguish between his accent (>) and short decrescendo mark (———). Furthermore, the two types of staccato markings (i.e. dots and wedges) have been confused by most earlier editors. This has occurred despite the fact that Schubert writes them quite differently. The dot is either a true dot or a short horizontal stroke, sometimes slanting. The wedge, on the other hand, is almost always a perfectly vertical stroke. Most often the dot appears in soft passages, the wedge in louder sections. To complicate the problem, Schubert frequently resorts to musical shorthand, furnishing the staccato marks only for the first notes of a passage—and then not always in every part that is affected.[5]

There is one rather important deviation from the manuscript to be found in the *Gesamtausgabe* and the many editions based on it. During the first movement a pedal B in the second bassoon and first horn (mm. 109–10 and mm. 327–28) has been altered to avoid a strong dissonance and to provide a conventional (i.e. dominant-to-tonic) cadence.

With respect to the sketches, no attempt has been made to alter Schubert's shorthand and in most cases even his mistakes have been allowed to stand. The latter are, for the most part, errors of omission (i.e. rests, accidentals, etc.). Correction would defeat the principal reason for possessing the sketches—namely, the intimate view of the composer in his workshop.

It may be noted, finally, that when Schubert writes *fp* ——— he actually intends the sound *f* ——— *p* (e.g. mm. 29–30 of the first movement).

The following list shows the significant points where the present edition diverges from the *Gesamtausgabe*. It does not, however, include the many places where Schubert's distinction between dot-staccato and wedge-staccato has been restored, or where such markings, missing in the *Gesamtausgabe,* have been reinstated.

Readings not in parentheses are those added in our edition; readings given in parentheses are those of the *Gesamtausgabe* that have been omitted (or replaced) here. As mentioned earlier, all such changes have been based on Schubert's autograph. Entries in italics explain other editorial emendations. It remains to be noted that Schubert's phrasing is often inconsistent.

4. Trombones are absent from Schubert's first six symphonies (1813–18), although they are occasionally to be found in his overtures (e.g. D. 12 and D. 26, both in D major). Schubert's use of three trombones (two tenors and a bass) for his last symphonies may be related to his fondness for Beethoven's Fifth, where, in the finale, trombones are used for the first time in Beethoven's symphonies. This is the only symphony by Beethoven predating the *Unfinished* to make use of three trombones. See the editor's essay, *Beethoven and the Unfinished,* p. 98 below.

5. See, for example, mm. 32–45 of the second movement. .

First Movement

20	Vn. I & II: decresc. starts on 4th eighth (5th eighth). *There is one of Schubert's rare extraneous markings,* ff, *over the third beat of Vn. I*
27	Ob., Cl., Bn., Hn., Va., Vcl., D.B.: cresc. begins with 1st beat (2nd beat)
	Fl.: cresc.
32–33	Winds, Vns.: cresc. over barline (on 3rd beat of m. 32)
	Va., Vcl., D.B.: cresc. on 6th eighth (5th eighth)
36	Trbs.: ff
63	D.B.: arco
67–68	Strings: decresc. ends on 1st beat of m. 68 (last beat of m. 67)
71	Woodwinds & Strings: ffz (fz).
95–97	Ob. I: slur from c² to d² & from f² to e² (one slur from b¹ to f², m. 96).
96–97	Bn. II: slur from g♯ to a & from b to c♯¹ (one slur from a to c♯¹, m. 97)
105	Winds: *p*
109	Bn. II: c♯¹ *has been erased in the autograph and replaced in Schubert's hand by B*
	Winds: accent (decresc.)
109–110a	Hn. I: a¹ (e¹)
110b	Winds: accent (decresc.)
136–39	Hns., Cl., Bn.: (accent)
170	Timp.: *this note written in another hand*
178, 182	Winds, Timp.: accent (decresc.)
184	Ob. II: 1st note f♯¹ (a¹)
190	Cl.: fz (f)
194	All: ff (ffz)
201	Hn.: d² dotted half, cresc. (rest)
208	Cl., Bn., Hn.: decresc.
213	Cl., Bn., Hn.: *pp* in middle of measure (beginning of m. 214)
232, 234	Fl. II, Ob. I: accents
238	Winds: cresc. on whole measure (on first 2 beats)
239	Winds: (decresc.)
241	Woodwinds & Strings: cresc. on 4th eighth (5th eighth)
243	Vn. I & II: decresc. on 2nd eighth, *p* on 3rd eighth (decresc. on 2nd & 3rd eighths, *p* on 4th eighth)
245	Vcl. & D.B.: *autograph gives last note as A, but see Va. and mm. 27, 31, 240*
246	Bn. I: last note d♯¹ (d¹)
246–47	Hn. I & II: (cresc.-decresc.)
247	Hn. I: 2nd beat, d² (f²)
277	Cl. I, Bn. II: (accent)
283	Vn. I: ffz *in the autograph*

286–87	Strings: cresc. starts on last beat of m. 286 (1st beat of m. 287)
290	Fl., Cl.: last note *p* (m. 291)
312	Vcl., D.B.: *pp* (*p*)
317	Vn. I & II: 2nd eighth count, *p*
319–20	Woodwinds & Strings: cresc. extends into m. 320; decresc. begins after 1st beat of m. 320 (decresc. begins on 1st beat of m. 320)
322–23	Winds: decresc. extends into m. 323; *p* middle of 323 (decresc. ends in m. 322; *p* beginning of 323)
324	Strings: pizz.
327	Bn. II: B (c♯)
	Winds: accent (decresc.)
327–28	Hn. I: a¹ (e¹)
328	Vcl., D.B.: arco
338	Vn. II: arco
340–43	Strings & Winds: accent (decresc.)
344	All: cresc. begins on 3rd beat (1st beat)
344 & 345	Vn. I & II: accent on 1st beat
345	Hn.: cresc. (m. 344)
346	Cl., Bn., Va.: slur starts on 2nd beat (1st beat)

Second Movement

14	D.B.: staccato
24	D.B.: slur begins from 1st beat (from 2nd beat)
27	Vn. I & II: slur ends here (last beat of m. 26)
32	*Strings: no "stacc." in autograph, but see parallel passage, m. 173*
35	Trb. I & II: (slur)
42	Woodwinds, Trb. I & II: (slur)
44–45	Fl. I: slur
45–47	Bn.: one slur over mm. 45–46, another over 47 (one slur over all 3 mm.)
48	Winds: decresc. (accent)
50	Winds, Timp., Vn. I & II, Va.: decresc. (accent)
54	Fl., Ob., Cl.: cresc. starts on 1st beat (2nd beat)
55	Vn. I & II: (decresc.)
56	D.B.: *pp*
58	D.B.: *ppp* (*pp*)
70–71	Cl.: cresc. in m. 71 only (begins in m. 70)
72	Vcl.: arco
73–74	Vn. I & II, Vcl.: *pp* on last note of m. 73 (1st beat of m. 74)
80–82	Cl.: decresc. in m. 80 & first half of m. 81 (m. 80 only); "morendo" at end of m. 81 (at beginning of m. 82)
85, 87	*Vcl.: these accents are not in the autograph; context and parallel passages indicate this to be an oversight*
96	D.B.: arco
99	Cl. I: (slur)

100	Fl. II, Ob. I, Cl. I & II: (slur)
101	Fl. II, Cl. II: (slur)
107	Bn. II: e (g)
109	All: ffz (fz)
120–21	Bn. II: slur from b to b (from b to c^1)
126–27	Vn. I: (tie)
	Vn. II: slur from last note of m. 126 to first of m. 127
127	Vn. II: slur on last 2 notes of measure (on last 3 notes)
127–29	Fl. II: slur from e^2 to g^2, another from c^3 to c^3
135	Hn.: (pp)
137	Hn.: pp
	Strings: decresc. (m. 136)
137–38	Va.: (slur between measures)
139–40	Vn. II: slur
173	Strings: ff on 1st beat (on 2nd beat); "stacc." marking here (in m. 175)
176	Trb. III: (stacc.)
191	Winds, Vn. I & II, Va.: decresc. for whole measure (accent)
	Vcl.: rest (plays with D.B.)
192	Vcl.: arco, p
211	Ob.: cresc. begins on last beat (after 1st note)
213–14	Ob., Strings: decresc. extends over barline (ends on last note of m. 213)
214	Vn. II: slur from $d\natural^1$ to db^1
214–15	Ob.: p in middle of m. 214, pp in middle of m. 215 (at beginning of respective mm.)
	Va.: slur from bb to a (slur from last note of 214 to 1st note of 215)
217	Ob.: (accent on 1st beat)
222–23	Ob.: morendo begins on last beat of m. 222 (1st beat)
230	Vcl.: accent and f on last note (f on 1st note of m. 231)
231–32	Strings: decresc. extends over barline (ends on last note of m. 231)
233	Strings: pp on 4th note (on 1st note)
241–42	Fl. II: slur from bb^2 to c^3 (from a^2 to a^2)
	Cl. I: (slur from c^2 to c^2)
250	Vn. II: ff on 1st beat
257, 259	Strings, Winds: decresc. (accent on first beat)
274	Vcl.: ppp
286–90	Bn. II: slur
288–89	Cl., Bn., Trb.: (cresc., decresc.)
289	Cl., Bn., Trb., Vn. II, Va.: accent on 1st beat
299	Winds: decresc. (accent on Fl. & Hn.)
301	Cl., Bn.: decresc. (accent)
303	Cl., Bn., Hn.: decresc. (accent)
305	Cl., Bn.: decresc. (accent)
308	Trb. I, II, III, Vcl.: ppp (pp)

ADDENDA (1971)

First Movement

41	Bn., Hn.: [*pp.* < >] *parallel with recapitulation:* cf. m. 255
63, 65	All: accent (decresc.)
67	All except Vn. I & II, Va.: accent (decresc.)
124, 128	Vn. I & II: accent (decresc.)
126	Bn., Va.: accent (decresc.)
128	Vn. II: cresc.
129	Vn. II: (cresc.)
130, 132	Vn. I: accents
146, 148, 154, 156, 162, 164, 196	All: accent (decresc.)
243	Vn. I & II: *fp* 2nd beat, decresc. marking 2nd beat to beginning m. 244; *parallel with exposition:* cf. m. 29–30 (decresc. 2nd part 1st beat)
256	Bn., Hn.: *pp, parallel with exposition:* cf. m. 42
281, 283	All: accent (decresc.)
285	All but Vn. I & II, Va.: accent (decresc.)
324–327	Vn. I & II, Va.: wedges, *parallel with exposition:* cf. mm. 106–110a.
324–328	Vcl., D.B.: wedges, *parallel with exposition:* cf. mm. 106–109.
327	Woodwinds, Hns.: accent (decresc.)
367	All: accent (decresc.)

Second Movement

12, 21, 27	Strings: accent (decresc.)
29	Fl. I, Bn., Hn., Vcl.: accent (decresc.)
31	Fl. I, Cl. I., Bn., Hn., Vcl.: accent (decresc.)
48	Fls., Cl. I., Bn. I.: accent (decresc.)
72	Strings: decresc. marking to end of measure (decresc. marking to 3rd beat)
147, 153	Strings: accent (decresc.)
162, 168	Strings, Bn. I.: accent (decresc.)
299	Fl., Cl., Hn., Vn. I & II.: accent (decresc.)
301	Cl., Bn., Hn. I., Vn. I & II.: accent (decresc.)
303	Cl., Bn., Hn.: accent (decresc.)
305, 307	Cl., Bn.: accent (decresc.)

The Piano Sketches

Schubert's piano sketches are here reprinted from the editorial commentary in the Schubert *Gesamtausgabe*. A few emendations have been made on the basis of a fresh comparison with the facsimile of the manuscript.

Numbers in brackets are those of the corresponding measures in the full score.

Passages in brackets are crossed out in the original.

* Schubert's repeat signs seldom have the dots.
** For some unexplained reason the d¹ has been erased and the a has been dotted.

* Schubert probably intended a¹-g♯¹-g♯¹, not b¹-a¹-a¹.

* *Sic*. Spacing indicates that Schubert intended eighth-notes.

* These four measures were inserted in the right-hand margin.

* Schubert intended either ♩ ♫♫ or ♩. ♫♫♫

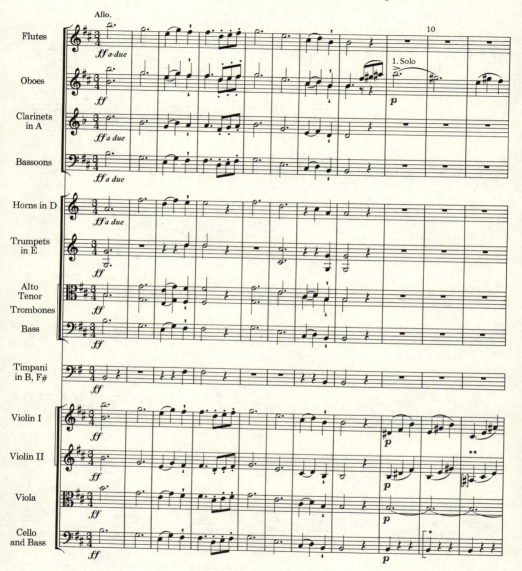

* See the article by Christa Landon, p. 130 below. Violoncello e Basso part omitted. Suggested line derived from
sketches.

** Possibly b rather than a[♯]. Sketch reads a♯.

Analysis

~~~~~~~

The First Movement

An excellent introduction to Schubert's movements in sonata form may be made with a contemporary description of that form by Carl Czerny. The Viennese Czerny (1791–1856), a child prodigy who studied with Beethoven, was a gifted pianist and an able composer, and became one of the most renowned pedagogues of his day. Beethoven entrusted his nephew Karl to Czerny for piano lessons; Franz Liszt was one of his pupils; and his piano methods are still used widely today. His extraordinarily numerous publications included solo piano arrangements of many songs and several overtures by Schubert. He also wrote a text on the subject of musical composition, entitled *Vollständige theoretisch-praktisch Kompositionslehre* (published by Diabelli in Vienna about 1840), in which there appeared, perhaps for the first time,[1] a completely accurate description of tripartite sonata form.

> The first movement consists of two parts, the first of which is usually repeated. This first part must comprise:
> 1. The principal subject.
> 2. Its continuation or amplification, together with a modulation into the nearest related key.
> 3. The middle subject in this new key.
> 4. A new continuation of this middle subject.
> 5. A final melody, after which the first part thus closes in the new key, in order that the repetition of the same [i.e., the first part] may follow unconstrainedly.
> The second part of the first movement commences with a development of the principal subject, or of the middle subject, or even of a new idea,

1. According to William S. Newman, *The Recognition of Sonata Form by Theorists of the Eighteenth and Nineteenth Centuries,* read before the American Musicological Society in 1941 and printed in *Papers of the A.M.S. for 1941* (1946).

First Movement: Allegro moderato

EXPOSITION *(First part)*

	First group		Trans.	Second group
Czerny:	*Principal subj.*		*Amplification & modul.*	*Middle subj.*
M.:	1	22	38	44
Key:	b		G	G
	(I)		(VI)	(VI)

DEVELOPMENT * *(Second part)*

|2.|

	Trans. (cont.)		Section I			Sequence I		
						⌐1¬	⌐2¬	⌐3¬
M.:	110	114		129	134	146	154	162
Key:	e			mod.	b	[c♯]	[d]	e
	(IV)				(I)	(II♯₅)	(III♮₃)	(IV)

RECAPITULATION ** *(Second part* cont.)

	First group (abr.)			Trans.		Second group	Ext.
Czerny:				*Amplification & modul.*		*Middle subj.*	
M.:	218	231		241		258	276
Key:	b	e	f♯	D		D	mod.
	(I)	(IV)	(V)	(III)		(III)	

CODA *

	Section I	Section II		▌
M.:	328	352	368	
Key:	b			
	(I)			

* Almost exclusively based on opening theme (mm. 1–8).
** Opening theme (mm. 1–8) omitted from Recapitulation; but see Coda.

|1.
:‖

		Closing section *Final melody*		Trans. or retrans.	
New cont. of middle subj.					
63	85	94		104	109
g	mod. G	G		b	
(VI)	(VI)	(VI)		(I)	

Section II   Retrans.

	Sequence II		Sequence III				
	⌐1¬	⌐2¬	⌐1¬	⌐2¬	⌐3→		
170	176	180	184	188	192	194	209
e	[b]	[f♯]	[b]	[e]			b
(IV)	(I)	(V)	(I)	(IV)			(I)

		Closing section *Final melody*	Trans.
Cont. of middle subj.			
281	303	312	322
b	mod. B	B	b
(I)	(I♯₃)	(I♯₃)	(I)

LEGEND

Major keys are identified by capital letters, minor by lower case.
Czerny's terminology is given in italics.
Brackets [ ] indicate tonal areas of temporary importance.
Figures in parentheses indicate relationship with the tonic, B minor.

M.	measure number	abr.	abridged
subj.	subject	ext.	extension
trans.	transition (bridge)	mod.	modulatory
modul.	modulation	retrans.	retransition
cont.	continuation		

passing through several keys, and returning again to the original key. Then follows the principal subject and its amplification, but usually in an abridged shape, so modulating, that the middle subject may likewise reappear entire, though in the original key; after which, all that follows the middle subject in the first part, is here repeated in the original key and thus the close is made.[2]

Certain aspects of Czerny's description are valuable for the analysis of sonata-form movements by Schubert and other 19th-century composers. Chief of these is his division of the first part (i.e. the exposition) into five sections. Most theorists, for example, ignore item 4 (i.e. the continuation of the middle subject) or refer to it only casually in passing. The diagram on pp. 72–73, however, indicates that for the exposition of the first movement of Schubert's *Unfinished* this section is of prime importance—the longest of the five, and by far the most exciting.

Also of interest is Czerny's term "middle subject" for item 3, a passage traditionally referred to as the second theme. In view of Schubert's many extensive expositions, the adjective "middle" is particularly fortunate. There is in the term a clear implication that important material is yet to follow. The term is especially apt for use in those expositions or recapitulations by Schubert where the middle (second) theme and the final (closing) section are in different keys.[3] Note, for example, the recapitulation as presented on the diagram.

Among other things, the diagram reveals that Schubert is more adventurous than is Czerny with respect to key sequence. He selects, for example, the submediant (G major) to provide the principal tonal contrast for the exposition, rather than the most closely related key suggested by Czerny.[4] In fact, it is in the recapitulation that Schubert makes use

---

2. *The School of Practical Composition*, transl. John Bishop, London, 1848, I, 33.

3. Where the first part of a sonata-form movement is concerned, the result is an exposition with three important and different key regions. In such cases—and with Schubert they are the rule rather than the exception—the key of the closing section is usually more closely related to the tonic than is the key of the middle theme. In the first movement of the Great C major Symphony (1828), for example, the exposition closes in the dominant (G major) although the middle theme begins in the key of the mediant (E minor). Structurally, the most important areas are the tonic key, in which the exposition begins, and the tonality of the closing group. Other keys are then heard primarily as passing. The temporary or passing quality is particularly emphasized by several of Schubert's middle themes that are modulatory; note, for example, the first movement of the Piano Trio in E♭ (Op. 100, 1827).

4. In minor this would have been either the relative major or the dominant (minor). Throughout his career Schubert preferred the submediant as his area of primary contrast for minor movements; see, for example, the outer movements of the Fourth ("Tragic") Symphony, D. 417.

of the more closely related tonalities. There are short passages in the subdominant (E minor) and dominant (F♯ minor) during the returning amplification of the first subject, and the relative major (D) serves as the key for the return of the second theme. It will be recalled that Czerny had specifically directed that the middle theme return in the original key.

Additional evidence of Schubert's more imaginative harmonic orientation is furnished by the "new continuation of the middle subject." At this point in the exposition no modulation is called for, since both second theme and closing section are in the same key. But the passage is modulatory, explosively so. If the function of the passage is not to facilitate a change of key, why is it here?

The answer to this question is to be found in Schubert's constant need for wide-ranging tonal movement, more distant key relationships, exciting harmonic progressions, and interesting vertical sonorities. For Schubert—and in this he is thoroughly Romantic—imaginative harmony is a primary concern. As a result, major formal divisions of his larger works, whether expository, developmental, or recapitulatory in function, usually include some tonal adventure. Or to put it another way, Schubert's ear could not tolerate extended passages completely in the tonic key. This is true despite the fact that most of the forms in which he chose to write (e.g. sonata form and rondo) evolved during the 18th century, when movements were generally shorter and there was less key movement. Returning sections, especially, tended at that time to appear in the tonic key. Schubert, however, seemed to feel that as long as the movement concluded in the key in which it began, he could—indeed, should—provide for the return of those musical aspects most significant to him. These included interesting (distant) relationships between adjacent keys or harmonies, tonal ambiguity, and an exciting manner of moving from one key to another.

In the first movement of the *Unfinished,* striking examples reflecting this attitude are provided by the transition to the key of the second theme and by the modulatory continuation of that same theme. These are two of the most effective passages in the entire exposition, and, although transposed, they are retained in their entirety for the recapitulation. In that section, however, Schubert has chosen the key of the relative major, D, for his second theme. In order to provide a transition that once more modulates down by the interval of a major third, he must conclude the returning amplification of the first theme in the key of F♯ minor.[5]

5. Exposition: B minor to G major; Recapitulation: F♯ minor to D major. Schu-

In similar fashion Schubert modifies the second theme so that the continuation could begin and end as before—that is, with the same tonic. In the exposition this had been G. However, in the recapitulation a return must be made from D major to B major. The necessary change of key is effected by a modulatory extension of the second theme *prior* to the continuation (mm. 276–79). The four-measure extension provides a modulation to the tonic, B minor, and the continuation itself now appears transposed but otherwise exactly as before (compare mm. 63–93 and mm. 281–311).

Another aspect of this continuation is noteworthy—its developmental quality. A comparison with the first half of the actual development section will indicate the similarity in structural approach.

1. Each of the comparable passages is tonally rounded: the continuation of the second theme begins in G minor and returns to G major; the first phase of the development begins and ends in E minor.
2. In each instance, the goal of the first modulation is the dominant (compare mm. 73–74 and m. 131 ff.).
3. The most important single element in both modulations proves to be a deceptive motion in the bass: the lowered sixth degree does not resolve to the dominant but instead rises chromatically (compare mm. 70–71 and 128–29).
4. Once the dominant has been reached, the return to the point of departure is achieved in similar fashion: by means of a modulating sequence. To be sure, the type of sequence differs; during the continuation of the middle theme the sequence stresses harmonic motion by fifth, whereas in the first part of the development the stages of the sequence are more extended and related by step.
5. In both passages there is an important reference to the syncopated chords first heard as preparation for the second theme. In each case the accompanying chords are heard without a melody—the frame without the picture, as it were—and yet in both instances the chords alone produce a brilliant effect (compare mm. 71–72 and mm. 150–69).
6. Each statement of the syncopation is preceded by a four-measure passage above a pedal bass, in which an arpeggio figures prominently. The arpeggio rises in the continuation, falls in the development. In fact,

bert also omits the first 8 measures of the exposition from the recapitulation, an omission that brings to mind his Fifth Symphony, in B♭ (D. 485, 1816). As in the present symphony, the first movement opens with an introductory element in the same tempo as the rest of the movement. The introduction is of great importance in the development and does not appear in the recapitulation. There, however, the parallel ends, since the recapitulation of the earlier work begins in the key of the subdominant, a favorite key for the point of recapitulation in Schubert's instrumental compositions dating from 1815–19.

the three statements of the arpeggio and syncopation in the development seem to have the effect of bringing to fruition an idea merely suggested in the earlier section.

At this point it may be appropriate to examine the variety of textures employed by Schubert. Four basic approaches may be discerned. The first consists of an unharmonized melody (e.g. mm. 1–8) or, at times, even a single tone (e.g. mm. 38–40). Such passages are often exploited by Schubert for their potential harmonic ambiguity.[6] In the development section and coda, for example, Schubert devotes much skill and energy to the task of presenting the unharmonized opening theme in a variety of harmonic and textural settings.

The second and most common texture for Schubert, as well as most other composers of the late 18th and 19th centuries, is that of a single melodic line with chordal accompaniment. As in the second theme (mm. 44–61), the chordal accompaniment may be rhythmically activated or, as in much keyboard music, the chords may be broken or embellished in some fashion.

Imitation plays a far smaller role in Schubert's music, although it occurs at crucial places in this movement (e.g. continuation of the second theme, mm. 73–84; closing section, mm. 94–104; development and coda). More often than not, only two real parts are involved. These two parts, however, are frequently reinforced by pedals (e.g. m. 122 ff.) or additional accompanying parts spelling out the harmonic implications of the imitated lines (e.g. m. 94 ff.). It may be observed that in Schubert's hands imitation is primarily a device for adding interest to a basically homophonic texture.[7]

The final approach, a stratified texture, is in many ways the most interesting for students of Schubert. Here the accompaniment consists of differentiated parts, each of which has a high degree of melodic and rhythmic independence. One of the most personal features of Schubert's mature style, this sort of texture appears to consist of layers or strata of sound. Because there is always a single, predominant melody, such a texture may be designated as "stratified homophony." In the first movement of the *Unfinished,* that portion of the primary group following the

6. See also the opening section of the fine Impromptu for Piano in C minor, Op. 90, No. 1 (D. 899, No. 1).

7. After his very earliest string quartets (e.g. the Quartet in Mixed Keys, D. 18), there are practically no fugues or fugatos in Schubert's music. In this respect he differs from Haydn, Mozart and Beethoven, all of whom composed occasional fugal movements, not to mention numerous fugatos, in their larger instrumental works.

opening phrase presents an unforgettable example of stratified homophony. As often happens with Schubert, the accompaniment is presented first (mm. 9–12). When the melody enters (m. 13 ff.), there are three lines differentiated with respect to melody, rhythm, register, and scoring.[8] As in many such passages by Schubert, doublings contribute much to the characteristically rich vertical sound.

The principal themes of this movement display Schubert's melodic powers at their height. Their sheer beauty and unforgettable quality defy analysis, but perhaps their interrelationships may be examined with profit.

The three notes ascending by step with which the composition begins (Ex. 1a, fig. x) are of primary importance. Rhythmically altered, the figure appears in the following accompaniment (Ex. 1b) and in the oboe and clarinet melody (Ex. 1c). The same ascent by step may be found in the middle theme, together with an increasingly important dotted-note variant (Ex. 1d). Schubert extracts from this theme the

Ex. 1   a)   mm. 1–8

b)   mm. 9–12

c)   mm. 13–20

8. See also the opening of the String Quartet in A minor, Op. 29 (D. 804, 1824).

d) mm. 44–47

e) mm. 63–66

f) mm. 94–99

g) mm. 122–25

single measure combining the dotted-note pattern and the ascending eighths (m. 46) for prominent use during the continuation of the middle theme (mm. 73–84). The melody of the closing section is closely derived from the middle theme and makes prominent use of the dotted-note figure (Ex. 1f). There is also a single reference to the eighth notes, now inverted. It is of interest to note that each time the eighth-note version occurs it does so on the last half of the measure; the dotted pattern, when present, invariably occupies the first beat.

A descending perfect interval, either fourth or fifth, provides another melodic element of importance. Present rather inconspicuously as a fourth in the opening bass melody (Ex. 1a, fig. y), the figure assumes primary importance as a falling fifth for the woodwind theme (Ex. 1c). In similar fashion, both middle and closing themes begin with the descending figure, now once more a perfect fourth (Ex. 1d and 1f). Note the appearance of this figure at the conclusion of each phrase of the middle theme. The relationship between perfect fourth and perfect fifth is made clear in these same concluding measures of the second theme (mm. 60–61) and in the first measures of the following continuation (Ex. 1e). In both instances, fourth is followed immediately by fifth or vice versa. It may be observed that the rhythm of the figure as it appears in the continuation (Ex. 1e) closely approximates that of the woodwind melody (Ex. 1c). The instruments chosen, high woodwinds, emphasize the relationship.[9]

Another interval of importance is the second (fig. z in Ex. 1), which is heard in both ascending and descending form (Ex. 1a and 1c) somewhat more frequently than figures previously discussed. Occasionally, the figure becomes that of a neighboring note (Ex. 1b and 1c). The most significant version, however, is that of the descending half step (e.g. Ex. 1g). See especially the development section (mm. 124–33) and the coda (mm. 340–47).

In addition to the unifying effect of the intervals discussed above, much of the consistency of the movement derives from the downbeat nature of each of the principal themes.[10] Of the many possible patterns available, Schubert places particular stress on the rhythm ♩ ♩. ♪ or its variant ♩ ♩ . This is also a downbeat figure, but with a marked emphasis on the second beat. First appearing inconspicuously in m. 18, figures accenting the second beat play an increasingly important role during the amplification of the first group. In fact, much of the rhythmic tension aroused in this amplification (m. 26 ff.) results from Schubert's brilliant opposition of the rhythm in question, played by the woodwinds and horns, to

9. Unfortunately, the sound of the descending intervals in Ex. 1a is lost in performance, one of Schubert's few miscalculations in scoring. He must have had fewer strings in mind but also underestimated the force of the brass. At the first performance the woodwinds were doubled in strength.

10. As Einstein has pointed out, Schubert "is what one might call a 'down-beat' composer, and even his up-beats are quiet." *Schubert,* New York, 1951, p. 250.

an equally powerful figure played by the lower strings. The latter rhythm avoids the second beat completely, ♩ ⅞ ♫♫ |(♩) .[11]

The accented second beat becomes a prime rhythmic element for the middle theme. Its dance-like character results from prominent use of the already-cited patterns stressing the second beat as well as the rhythmic placement of an ascending dotted figure on the first beat. As a result, the second beat carries both the high point of the figure itself and the high points of the entire phrase.

It has been suggested that the origin of the middle theme is to be found in a Viennese street song still heard in the 20th century. The music is in two parts, with both claiming equal melodic significance; if there is only one singer he may sing either part as a solo. Notice particularly the similarity of measures 3 and 4 of the lower part to the opening measures of Schubert's theme.[12]

The emphasis on the second beat is equally prominent during the second theme and the closing section. It may be remarked that an effective rhythmic foil to the stressed second beat is provided by the constantly syncopated accompanying chords present in both middle and closing sections. It should also be noted that chords in the same syncopated rhythms, but without a melody, occur at climactic moments during the continuation of the middle theme (mm. 71–72) and the development section (m. 150 ff.). The syncopated chords return to an accompanying role later in the continuation (mm. 81–84).

The first beat again assumes primary importance during the transition leading to the development section (m. 105 ff.). Since the development is almost exclusively concerned with the opening theme or melodic

11. Ludwig Misch traces the rhythm of this particular figure in twenty songs and a number of instrumental compositions by Schubert in *Ein Lieblingsmotiv Schuberts,* in *Die Musikforschung,* XV (1962), 146. Included among the songs mentioned by Misch are several in B minor. Mosco Carner in his fine chapter on "The Orchestral Music," in the volume entitled *The Music of Schubert,* New York, 1947, also mentions these B minor songs, especially *Suleika I,* written a year prior to the *Unfinished* (1821). A bass motif in *Suleika I* closely resembles the bass motif cited above.

12. Example cited from Walther Vetter, *Der Klassiker Schubert,* Leipzig, 1953, p. 278.

ideas derived therefrom, the rhythmic emphasis remains on the first beat.
Significantly, a single idea from the latter portions of the exposition is
heard in the development, and this proves to be the only element without an emphasis on the second beat—the syncopated accompanying
chords (mm. 150–69). These chords appear as in the continuation of
the second theme—that is, without a primary melody.

For his first movement Schubert seems to have developed an interesting rhythmic design of alternating sections. Completely absent from
the beginning of the work (mm. 1–17), figures emphasizing the second
beat grow in importance during the remainder of the exposition. They
are absent again from the largest portion of the development, return
during the recapitulation, and are once more absent from the coda.

The first section of the piano sketches for this movement were lost
sometime in the 19th century. The remaining portion begins during the
recapitulation, at a point corresponding to m. 250 of the full score.
Comparison of the fragmentary sketches with the orchestral version reveals a number of interesting features. Schubert's concise, masterly transition to the key of the second theme, for example, appears as a far more
prosaic affair in the sketches:

Furthermore, Schubert modulates to B major in the recapitulation
during the continuation of the second theme. Consequently, the four
measures extending the second theme (mm. 276–79) are absent from
the sketches and the continuation itself differs from both the expository
and recapitulatory versions of the orchestral score. Finally, the coda is
a shorter, less interesting section with no references to the poignant variant of the opening measures used so effectively by Schubert during the
development and coda of the orchestrated version. In contrast with the
first movement, there are no significant differences between the two versions of the second movement.

The Second Movement

The choice of key for the slow movement, E major, results in an unusual relationship to that of the first movement: the opposite mode of the subdominant.[13] There is no direct precedent for this among Schubert's instrumental works, although there are other examples of distant relationships. The closest of these are two sonatas, both in A minor, that have slow movements in the opposite mode of the dominant.[14] Interestingly enough, the key of those movements is identical with that of the *Unfinished:* E major. The same key was selected by Schubert for the slow movement of his single larger work in B major, the Piano Sonata, Op. 162 (D. 574)—not an unusual choice in this case. Clearly, then, it is not the key itself that is unusual for Schubert, but its relationship with the tonic of the first movement and with the B minor of the fragmentary scherzo that follows. Can we better understand Schubert's choice? Possibly.

Maurice J. E. Brown has pointed to the conclusion of the first movement of the piano sketches, a chord of B major. He may very well be correct in hypothesizing that such an ending "would have both indicated and justified the choice of key for his slow movement." [15] However, the same sketches and the nine orchestrated measures of the third movement indicate that Schubert planned to return directly to B minor after the slow movement. The same unusual relationship would then occur.

There is another possible explanation. One of the most strikingly effective melodic ideas of the entire movement occurs in the opening measures: a poignant descending bass line played against slowly rising chords. The passage derives a large degree of its effectiveness from the scoring, and here may be found a reason for Schubert's choice of key. The falling line is scored for double basses playing pizzicato. The lowest note

13. As first pointed out by Ernst Laaff, *Schuberts h-moll Symphonie,* in *Gedenkschrift für H. Abert,* Halle, 1928, the principal themes of the two completed and one fragmentary movement are related. See the essay on "Beethoven and the Unfinished," p. 98 below.

14. The Piano Sonata, Op. 164 (D. 537) and the Sonata for Arpeggione, D. 821.

15. *Essays on Schubert,* New York, 1966, p. 10.

of the descending figure is the lowest note that can be performed on the usual four-string double bass, the instrument with which Schubert was familiar, an open-string E.[16] The combined figures, descending scale and rising chords, recur several times in the movement, usually with the same scoring.[17] Had Schubert chosen the key of the relative (D major), this figure would not have been possible without distorting its shape or rescoring the line for cellos. In either case much of the effect would have been lost. Similarly, the line would have been less effective if the movement had been written in a higher key—for example, that of G major, the key of the submediant.

If the choice of key is unusual, the form is not. It is a favorite of Schubert's—an extended bipartite movement suggesting a variety of sonata form. Schubert's handling of this form is individual, but it may be profitably compared with two related forms originating in the 18th century.

The first and older of the two is commonly labeled bipartite sonata form and consists of a pair of approximately equivalent sections, each of which is repeated. During part one there is a modulation from the tonic to a closely related area, and in the second part there is a return to the original key for the close. The subject matter of the new key in the first part may or may not be similar to that with which the movement began. Actually, the most consistent thematic resemblances are usually between the cadence passages concluding each part.

The second type has been labeled sonata form without development or, more concisely, abridged sonata form. In this type, developed later than bipartite sonata form, each of the two parts is more extended. Because of the greater scope and a more dramatic orientation, there is usually a more consistent thematic differentiation coordinated with the changes of key—that is, new and contrasting subject matter helps to mark the advent of the second key area. At the conclusion of the first part (i.e. the exposition) there is a retransition to the original key for the beginning of the second part (i.e. the recapitulation). The return of thematic materials takes place, for the most part, in the tonic key. The composer may call for a repetition of the first part or, less often, of both parts, and he may also include an introduction or coda or both. Without repeats this form was often used for overtures by composers of

16. See, for example, the contemporary discussion of the "Contra-Basso" in Augustin Sundelin, *Die Instrumentierung für das Orchester,* Berlin, 1828, pp. 8–10.
  17. See mm. 7–9, 58–60, 142–44 and 148–50.

Italian operas during the late 18th or early 19th century.[18] Schubert became familiar with many such overtures as a violinist and assistant conductor of the orchestra at the Vienna City Seminary. As a boy he also wrote many overtures with this form for orchestra and other instrumental media.[19]

It is not surprising, therefore, that a number of Schubert's slow movements, including that of the *Unfinished*, closely resemble the abridged sonata form without repeats. As with his first movement, this one differs from those of his predecessors and contemporaries largely with respect to tonal organization (see the diagram on p. 86).

It may be observed that in the recapitulation the final portion of the secondary thematic group (m. 112 ff.) is replaced by a passage based on a cadential element belonging to the primary thematic section (m. 257 ff.). Most importantly, the larger portion of the recapitulation is in the key of the subdominant, A major, or in the opposite mode of the subdominant, A minor. As a result, the coda (m. 268 ff.) has an unusually important tonal function. It helps to provide the necessary tonic orientation lacking earlier.

The rounded design of the first group of themes (A A' B A'') is noteworthy, and typical of Schubert's opening sections in lyric movements. The initial passage (mm. 1–16) recurs immediately, with a most interesting tonal alteration (mm. 16–32). Following a modulatory passage of only partially contrasting thematic material (mm. 33–45), the original constellation of melodic ideas is heard once more, although the order of thematic elements has been changed (mm. 45–60). In this final passage, the introductory measures (mm. 1–3) are utilized to close the group (mm. 56–60).

As so often in Schubert's music, the modulatory scheme provides the most interesting feature of the formal design. During A' there is a sudden but effective modulation to the region of the lowered submediant, G major (mm. 18–26). The manner of achieving the change of key is a direct one, and a favorite procedure for Schubert's excursions to distant areas. The tonic chord is altered to minor (m. 18) and treated as the submediant of the new key.

This is only one of a number of modulations in the *Unfinished* in-

18. See, for example, Mozart's overture to *The Marriage of Figaro,* or various overtures by Rossini.

19. See Martin Chusid, *Schubert's Overture for String Quintet and Cherubini's Overture to Faniska,* in *Journal of the American Musicological Society,* XV (1962), 78–84.

Second Movement: Andante con moto

EXPOSITION

First group

	A	A′	B			A″	cad.
M.:	1	17	33	37	41	45	56
Key:	E	G		[B]	[c♯]	E	
	(I)	(bIII)		(V)	(VI)	(I)	

Trans. Second group

		mod.							Trans.	
M.:	62	64	82	96	111	118	125			
Key:	c♯	c♯	D♭	c♯	D	[G]	[C]			
	(VI)	(VI)	(VI♯3)	(VI)	(bVII)	(bIII)	(bVI)			

Retrans.

M.:	130	135 mod.

RECAPITULATION

First group

	A	A′	B	A″	cad.
M.:	142	158	174	186	197
Key:	E	G	[f♯]	A	
	(I)	(bIII)	(II)	(IV)	(I)

Trans. Second group (slightly abridged)

		mod.				Trans.	
M.:	203	205	223	237	244	257	260
Key:	a	a	A	a	e	(A)	E
	(IV♭3)	(IV♭3)	(IV)	(IV♭3)	(I♭3)		(I)

CODA

Section I

	(A)
M.:	268
Key:	E
	(I)

Section II

			Trans.	(A)
M.:	280	286	290	296
Key:	E	A♭		E
	(I)	(III♯3)		(I)

LEGEND

Major keys are identified by capital letters, minor keys by lower case.
Brackets [ ] indicate tonal areas of temporary importance.
Figures in parentheses indicate relationship with the tonic, E major.

M.	measure number
cad.	cadences
trans.	transition (bridge)
mod.	modulatory
retrans.	retransition

dicating Schubert's predilection for emphasizing areas either a third above or below the tonic. Most often these are related regions, as in the first movement (i.e. G major—VI of B minor—and D major—III), or in the second group of the second movement (i.e. C♯ minor as VI of E major). However, frequently chromatic alterations occur, as here, and help to provide an expanded range of available keys.

A favorite harmonic procedure of Schubert's facilitates modulations by thirds. He reharmonizes one or, less often, several notes in a new and often unexpected key. In the example initiating this discussion, the first note of the melodic line in the upper strings, b′ (m. 18), is approached as if it were the fifth degree of the scale of E but left as the third degree of the scale of G. Compare also the frequently cited transition to the second key area in the first movement. An unharmonized d′ (m. 38 ff.) suggests the third degree of B minor with reference to the preceding full close in that key, but as the principal agent in the modulation to G major it is treated as the fifth degree of the new key.[20] Schubert's fondness for melodic ideas stressing the third or sixth degree of the scale facilitates such modulations.

The principal melodic elements in this movement are, in order of importance: scale passages (e.g. mm. 1–3 melody and bass), outlined triads or seventh chords (e.g. mm. 5, 15, 90 ff.), and the interval of a third (e.g. mm. 2, 4, 33, and 35 bass line, and especially m. 66 ff.).

The texture is rich, and as in the first movement Schubert uses a variety of approaches. There is, however, a marked emphasis on duets between the outer voices; see especially the entire first group of themes (mm. 1–60), and mm. 84–89 of the second group. The duets usually involve notably differentiated melodic ideas, but there is an effective example of Schubert's approach to imitation in two parts during the second group (m. 113 ff.). This passage follows on the most exciting outburst of the movement (mm. 96–108). Here invertible counterpoint is suggested by the transfer to the bass of the principal melody of the group.

20. Several times in works from the last year of his life, Schubert harmonizes, to brilliant effect, a segment of a melodic line in two keys. The second statement follows immediately on the first, and its key is removed by a third from the tonic. See the opening sections in the slow movements of the Piano Sonatas in A major (D. 959) and B♭ major (D. 960).

THE PROBLEM
OF THE "UNFINISHED"

Unless specified otherwise, all numbered footnotes in the following essays are those of the author.

OTTO ERICH DEUTSCH[†]

The Riddle of
Schubert's Unfinished Symphony

Only after this title had appeared in the prospectus of *The Music Review* did the writer recollect that a similar title had been given to one of the two pamphlets which have recently discussed the Unfinished Symphony, *Franz Schubert's Symphonie in h-moll (Unvollendete) und ihr Geheimnis*.[1] For this reason the reader must be warned at the outset that here no mysteries will be solved and the riddle which this work of Schubert's presents to us can be only partially explained. This is, perhaps, fortunate since the mystery that surrounds the B minor Symphony is one of the main causes of its influence. There was no reason for Schubert to have left us an account of the original plan of the work which at any rate was not intended as programme music, and he has not explained why he left it with only two movements.

* * *

Why Schubert left the work unfinished can only be conjectured. One of the Schubert films goes so far in legend and fiction as to give as the cause, the marriage of the countess Karolina Esterhazy.[2] Walter Dahms, in his biography of Schubert (second edition, 1918, p. 130), writes: "The Unfinished Symphony seemed to its creator himself, sufficiently finished for him to dispense with the completion of the usual plan of a Symphony —a concession to average æsthetic standards." Paul Mies endeavours thus to explain the interruption of the Symphony: "Something had interrupted Schubert in the course of the composition and he was unable to recover the sense of unity. He preferred leaving it unfinished to bringing it to an

---

[†] From *The Music Review,* I (1940), 36–53; translated by Dr. K. Wood-Legh; reprinted by permission. Some sections have been omitted.

1. By Arnold Schering, published in Würzburg, 1939. Deutsch's discussion of the second pamphlet, the work of an "amateur," is omitted here. [*Editor*]

2. This music pupil of Schubert's was twelve years old when he went for the first time to the Hungarian castle of Zseliz in 1818, thus in 1824 she was eighteen, and did not marry until after his death.

end without such unity." (*Zeitschrift für Musikwissenschaft,* November 1924.) Hans Mersmann believed that Schubert was inwardly broken by the attempt to unite the contrasts in this work. (*Die moderne Musik seit der Romantik,* 1927.) Ernst Laaff wrote, in 1928, that Schubert was wrecked by the Scherzo, because he wished to avoid the common type, and later succeeded in avoiding it, in the Octet and in the Great C major Symphony. Walter Vetter seems to have said the last word on this for our time, "There is no more fundamental misunderstanding of the type of Schubert's work than to suppose that he aimed at developing a new kind of symphony in two movements. The B minor Symphony is beyond doubt a fragment." (*Franz Schubert,* Potsdam, 1934.)

There can be no thought of Schubert's having deliberately limited his work to two movements. But the authorities concur in the opinion that in this work there is something entirely new, not only in Schubert's compositions, but for all music. "The B minor Symphony bursts the bonds of tradition. Both in form and content, it presents something entirely new, something unique which after the death of Schubert was never again to be achieved." Thus writes Vetter, but as early as 1882, George Grove says in his Dictionary, "in them, . . . for the first time in orchestral composition, Schubert exhibits a style absolutely his own, untinged by any predecessor, and full of that strangely direct appeal to the hearer. . . . At length, in the B minor Symphony, we meet with something which never existed in the world before in orchestral music—a new class of thoughts and a new mode of expression which distinguish him entirely from his predecessors, characteristics which are fully maintained in the *Rosamunde* music ([Fall] 1823), and culminate in the Great C major Symphony (March, 1828)." *** On still another occasion Grove wrote of this work when it was performed on October 3rd, 1900, at the Birmingham Musical Festival (Introduction to the Programme, p. 42 ff.): "In no other piece of music, perhaps, is the feeling so entirely produced that one has been in communication with the very person of the composer himself."

"The first movement is sadly full of agitation and distress," says Grove in 1882. And Ludwig Scheibler about 1914 added (in an unpublished revision of a German translation of Grove's biography[3]), "The second movement dreams of the pastures of the blessed. One is reminded of a poetic allegory. Usually the symphony is interpreted as a certain

---

3. Deutsch is undoubtedly referring to the lengthy article on Schubert that Grove wrote for his *Dictionary of Music and Musicians.* [*Editor*]

premonition of death and a vision of heaven." But with regard to this it should be observed that Schubert's serious illness did not begin till the end of 1822, thus after his work on the B minor Symphony which he had certainly finished by the middle of November—and that it is not until later that we hear his first complaints of loneliness. Still more important, perhaps, is Scheibler's suggestion of a hermeneutic exposition which the last year has offered to us, in the pamphlet by Arnold Schering, of Berlin, cited at the beginning of this article. This author formerly explained Beethoven's Ninth Symphony by certain poems of Schiller, and still earlier five string quartets and eight piano sonatas, by various Shakespeare plays. There is an old German proverb which may perhaps justify the illustrated Bible, *Was G'lehrte durch die Schrift verstan, Das weist das G'mäl dem g'meinen Mann.* (What the scholar understands from the written words, pictures show to the common man.) Contrariwise one might say of such a tendency to explain masterpieces of music— What the ordinary man can easily perceive through his ear, the scholar must explain to himself with carefully selected words. In discussing the works of Beethoven, moreover, Professor Schering has sought both for their inspiration and for the subjects of individual themes in many literary classics, both German and foreign, even though there is no evidence that Beethoven so much as knew of their existence. In fact the acquisition of so wide a knowledge of literature as Professor Schering assumes Beethoven to have possessed would have made such demands upon his energies that his own creative work must have been greatly diminished. Further, however wide may be the literary knowledge of an individual scholar, what it includes must to some extent be determined by chance and thus any attempt to explain musical compositions thereby is inevitably dangerous.

But with regard to Schubert, the Berlin scholar has been exceptionally fortunate. There is an allegorical tale by him, *Mein Traum*,[4] bearing the date 3rd July, 1822, thus four months earlier than that of the Symphony score. This narrative, which apparently refers to some personal experiences of the young man, Dahms, with the aid of material supplied by his fellow-worker Alois Fellner of Vienna, has used with great ingenuity in writing his biography of Schubert.[5] Fellner assumes that Schubert's father, considering that music was taking too much of his son's attention from his ordinary studies while he attended the *Stadtkonvikt*

4. *SR*, No. 298. [*Editor*]
5. Walter Dahms, *Schubert*, Berlin and Leipzig, 1912. [*Editor*]

as a chorister, had forbidden him his house and that it was only in 1812 at his mother's funeral that the fifteen-year-old Franz was reconciled to his father. For this, however, there is no historical evidence; it is only a hypothesis based on the narrative of the dream. The lack of other support for this theory renders the whole of Fellner's interpretation of the tale doubtful. And consequently Dahms, though accepting the theory as to Schubert's father, already omitted the explanation of the allegory in the second edition *** of his book. Although Schering has cited only the fourth edition *** Fellner's theory is still accepted.[6]

Schering found the allegory divided into two parts and in the first part, "which has the construction of the usual sonata form," the "reprise" even gives evidence of a second dismissal from his father's house. The second part, "the account of the vision," "proceeds like the thematic development of the *Andante*." Thus Schubert, the poet, has himself shown us why the Symphony could have only two movements: the libretto was insufficient for more. Schering, moreover, believes that "the historians of music of the next fifty years" will have to seek "the poetic foundations of Schubert's other instrumental masterpieces." It is to be hoped that in this time there will also be the humour needed for such a task.

*   *   *

Another hypothesis of Dahms is that Schubert endeavoured to become a member of the Vienna *Gesellschaft der Musikfreunde* in order, if possible, to have his B minor Symphony performed by this Society. Apart from the fact that at that time there was no talk of such works between Schubert and his supporters in this musical Society, and in spite of the difficulties which stood in the way of a professional musician's admission to this Society of amateurs, he was already a member. The programme of a concert of 18th November, 1821, describes him as a member of the Society and a list of members compiled in 1844 shows him to have been enrolled in March, 1822 (*Anbruch,* Vienna, December, 1937). The tradition that at the end of 1822, Schubert tried in vain to become a member is, moreover, rendered incredible by the evidence of a directory of Vienna artists printed at the beginning of 1823, which mentions him as a pianist and viola player, among the active members of the Society. But whilst the Vienna *Gesellschaft der Musikfreunde* elected

6. One argument of Fellner's is clearly false. He quotes the postscript of Schubert's letter written on 2nd November, 1821, to Josef v. Spaun, from Kreissle's biography: *Schreibe recht bald an den Vater.* In the original this is *an Patr.,* which stands not for *Patrem* but for the Patriarch of Venice, who was then the poet Ladislaus Pyrker v. Felsö-Eör, an error which Fellner's father-complex has led him to retain.

him to its representative Committee only about the middle of 1827, he was chosen an honorary member of the *Steiermärkischer Musikverein* in Graz in the spring of 1823, and of the *Linzer Gesellschaft der Musikfreunde* in the autumn of the same year at the latest.

*   *   *

On 8th March, 1860, Joseph Hüttenbrenner, then *Adjunkt* in the Ministry of the Interior, wrote to the Kapellmeister Johann Herbeck *** In this letter, Joseph asked for a ticket for a concert and for his appointment as *Primo Tenore assoluto;* but as a fanatical devotee of his brother whose merits he greatly over-estimated, he also used the opportunity to recommend for performance Anselm's songs—"which can be unhesitatingly acclaimed as the true successors of the Schubert songs"—his quartets, choruses, operas, overtures, symphonies, masses and requiems. At the end of this wordy letter, he offers this bait to Herbeck: "He [Anselm] possesses a treasure in Schubert's B minor Symphony which we rank with his Great C major Symphony, his instrumental swan song, and with all the symphonies of Beethoven—only it is unfinished. Schubert gave it to me for Anselm to thank him for having sent the diploma of the Graz Music Society through me. Anselm also has the original score of Mozart's *Bergknappen-Sinfonie*." [7]

In 1863, the Unfinished Symphony was first mentioned in print: C. v. Wurzbach's *Biographisches Lexikon des Kaisertums Österreich* contained, in volume IX, a biography of Anselm Hüttenbrenner, the material for which Joseph had helped to furnish. This biography twice mentions as in Anselm's possession the Symphony which Schubert had dedicated to him and which he had arranged for four hands. Not until two years later, after Kreissle had referred to it in his great biography of Schubert and urged Anselm no longer to withhold it from the public, did Herbeck venture to visit him. Anselm at that time was living in Ober-Andritz

---

7. This is the *Musikalischer Spass* (*Köchels Verzeichnis*, No. 522), also called the *Bauern-Sinfonie*. Weber describes the peasant music with which his *Freischütz* begins as *böhmische Bergmusik*. In 1834 the Vienna periodical *Hans Jörgel* wrote of the music of the *reisende Bergknappen* (travelling miners) and as late as 1870 the itinerant musicians with their wind-instruments were called in Mainz *Bergknappen* on account of their costume. The manuscript of Mozart's Sextet, which in reality parodies bad composers not performers, Anselm Hüttenbrenner had received as a gift from Schubert after they had played it on the piano. The latter had been given it by Mozart's little-known friend the physician, Dr. Anton Schmidt. Schubert wanted to divide the manuscript with Anselm, but when he opposed the division Schubert gave him the whole. The manuscript has now disappeared. This work as well as the B minor Symphony Anselm arranged for four hands, perhaps stimulated by his playing with Schubert.

near Graz and had become an eccentric, pious, seeking to forget his youth, occupied with theology and magnetism, discontented with the reception his works had received and distrustful, especially of strangers. To overcome this, Herbeck took advantage of an opportunity of accompanying his sister-in-law who was ill on her journey to Meran, and carefully planned a way of getting in touch with him without arousing his suspicion. On the morning of the 1st May, 1865, Herbeck arrived in the village and, finding that the inn where he had gone by chance was the one which the Styrian musician daily frequented, awaited him there. "I have come," he said when Hüttenbrenner arrived, "to ask you to allow one of your compositions to be performed in Vienna." Anselm thereupon escorted Herbeck to his home the *Strasserhof* and into his study that looked like a lumber-room. Furniture, including a closed stool, had to be pushed out of the way before all the manuscripts could be reached and spread out—first, of course, those of Anselm himself. Herbeck while still in Vienna had chosen for the performance Anselm's Overture in C minor (one of his three concert-overtures), and had obtained the manuscript from Joseph, but now he also took from Anselm two overtures to plays. This being settled, Herbeck said, "I intend to bring the three contemporaries, Schubert, Hüttenbrenner and Lachner before the Vienna public in a single concert. Naturally I would like very much to have Schubert represented by a new work." Anselm replied, "Well, I still have a lot of things by Schubert." Then from a drawer crammed with papers in an old-fashioned chest, he pulled out the symphony. Herbeck maintained his outward calm while he held the desired manuscript in his hand, turned over its pages and gradually realised the beauty of the work. "That would be quite suitable" he said, then with consummate diplomacy, "will you allow me to have the manuscript transcribed immediately at my expense?" But Anselm, who had been completely won over, replied "There is no need to hurry, you are welcome to take it with you." Later, Anselm wrote on Herbeck's visiting card ". . . called on me on the morning of the 1st May, 1865, in *Strasserhof*. Entrusted to him for performance: the original manuscript of Schubert's B minor Symphony, also the overtures to *Armella,* to the *Räuber* and some songs! I empowered him to perform my C minor Overture for the benefit of Schubert's poor relations." So these manuscripts, the decoy and the game, arrived on that very day in Vienna where the Schubert manuscript, after its long exile, was henceforth to remain. From Herbeck it passed to the collector, Nikolaus Dumba, and after his death, in 1900, to the archives of the *Gesell-*

schaft der Musikfreunde, together with five of the six symphonies of Schubert's youth.

*   *   *

And now a word as to musical opinion after Schubert's death. In the last seventy years it has made up for the neglect of which Schubert's friend was guilty. Schubert himself who had abandoned the Symphony and had given it away unconditionally as a token of gratitude and remembrance to Anselm Hüttenbrenner would certainly be astonished to hear that it has now become the favourite of the world. This is in some small measure due to the unpleasant handiwork of Herr Berté and his associates who through the *Dreimäderlhaus* ("Lilac Time") and its successors, have popularised Schubert in so painful a manner that the B minor Symphony has even been turned into jazz. One of the numerous Schubert films (as has been mentioned above) has also contributed towards this.

Thus it is not surprising that in 1928 the Columbia Graphophone Company considered offering a prize for the best completion of the Unfinished Symphony. But their representative's visit to Vienna in connexion with this plan led to the adoption of a better course. The first prize, which was won by the Swede, Atterberg, was for the best new symphony after the manner of Schubert. But a smaller prize offered for the discovery of the lost *Gmunden-Gasteiner Sinfonie* failed to achieve its purpose. After J. Joachim had arranged the Grand-Duo Op. 140 as a symphony and J. F. Barnett had completed the score sketch of the E major Symphony an attempt was made, in 1892, to finish the Unfinished Symphony: the Saxon, August Ludwig, crowned Schubert's work with a "Philosophical Scherzo" as a third movement and a "March of Fate" as a fourth. The year 1928, despite the change in the purpose of the Columbia prize, produced four further attempts including one by Frank Merrick. W. Vetter, in his biography of Schubert, states that F. v. Weingartner finished the B minor Symphony, whereas, in reality he had only made a more successful attempt to complete the E major sketch. Equally incorrect is the statement by C. Reinecke in Spemann's *Goldenes Buch der Musik* of 1900, that N. Gade's Eighth Symphony in B minor contained two movements which were originally intended to be added to Schubert's Symphony. This has been proved by Herbert F. Peyser in his valuable article "The Epic of the Unfinished," published in *The Musical Quarterly,* New York, October, 1928.

MARTIN CHUSID

~~~~~~

Beethoven and the Unfinished

The influence of Beethoven's orchestral music on important 19th-century composers such as Berlioz, Wagner, and Brahms has long been recognized. In fact discussions of their music often take their point of departure from Beethoven's symphonic legacy. There has been much less discussion of Schubert's orchestral works in these terms and yet Beethoven's young contemporary was fully as much in his debt as were later composers.[1]

Some of the most convincing evidence for this statement is to be found in Schubert's own words. Two of the seventy letters by Schubert still extant mention compositions by Beethoven and in both cases it is the orchestral works that are stressed.

The first letter was written as a result of a pledge. Apparently Schubert had agreed to provide a composition for orchestra to a conductor tentatively identified by Otto Erich Deutsch as one of his former teachers at the Imperial Seminary. As a choir boy in the Royal Chapel, Schubert received his schooling at the Seminary from 1808 to 1813. During this time he played violin in the active Seminary orchestra and after a while became the assistant conductor as well. He was much devoted to the group, and for several years after his departure he is reported to have revisited the school, often bringing compositions that he had just completed for performance and criticism. The letter reads:

1. It has never been conclusively established that Beethoven and Schubert met formally. It is of interest to note, however, that Schubert is mentioned three times in Beethoven's conversation books from the years 1823 to 1826. These entries are reproduced in *SR*, pp. 288, 341, and 536. Because of Beethoven's deafness his visitors were compelled to write out their part of the conversation. The three visitors mentioning Schubert are Beethoven's nephew Karl, Anton Schindler (1794–1864), and Karl Holz (1798–1858), for some time second violinist in Schuppanzigh's quartet. Schindler was, of course, Beethoven's first biographer. Holz was an intimate friend and also served as a copyist for Beethoven. Beethoven intended that Holz should write his biography.

[undated]

Most valued Herr von Bäutel,

Since I actually have nothing for full orchestra which I could send out into the world with a clear conscience, and there are so many pieces by great masters, as for instance Beethoven's Overture to 'Prometheus,' 'Egmont,' 'Coriolanus,' &c. &c. &c., I must very cordially ask your pardon for not being able to oblige you on this occasion, seeing that it would be much to my disadvantage to appear with a mediocre work. Forgive me, therefore, for having accepted too rashly and unthinkingly.

Your most devoted,

Frz. Schubert.[2]

The second letter was written in 1824 during preparations for a concert entirely devoted to Beethoven's music. At this important event the Ninth Symphony, portions of the *Missa Solemnis,* and the Overture *Consecration of the House* received their first performances.

During the preceding winter Schubert began to meet regularly with Ignaz Schuppanzigh and other musicians close to Beethoven. Schuppanzigh, organizer and leader of the first professional string quartet, was also concertmaster for the performance of the Ninth. He and members of his quartet had taken part in the première performances of almost all of Beethoven's concerted music with strings, and they were now beginning to interest themselves in Schubert's music as well. In fact Schuppanzigh's quartet had performed Schubert's A minor Quartet, Op. 29, for the first time in public on March 14, just seventeen days prior to the letter, and Schubert dedicated the work to Schuppanzigh. The letter was addressed to a friend, Leopold Kupelwieser, who was at that time in Rome. In part, it reads:

March 31, 1824

Dear Kupelwieser,

. . . Of songs I have not written many new ones, but I have tried my hand at several instrumental works, for I wrote two Quartets for violins, viola and violoncello and an Octet, and I want to write another quartet, in fact I intend to pave my way towards grand symphony in that manner. —The latest in Vienna is that Beethoven is to give a concert at which he is to produce his new Symphony, three movements from the new Mass and a new Overture.—God willing, I too am thinking of giving a similar concert next year. . . .

Your

faithful Friend

Frz. Schubert.[3]

2. *SR,* No. 345. Deutsch suggests 1823 as a possible date for the letter.
3. *SR,* No. 456. The two quartets already written by Schubert were the A minor,

The almost naive desire to emulate Beethoven is touching, and the juxtaposition of thoughts expressed leaves no doubt that Schubert means "grand symphony" in Beethoven's manner. But which of Beethoven's symphonies did he have in mind? Which of them were most familiar to him? Which were his favorites?

We are fortunate in having a large collection of memoirs concerning Schubert written by his friends and published by Otto Erich Deutsch. Several of these memoirs contain discussions of orchestral groups in which Schubert performed. Anton Holzapfel (1792–1868), "an enthusiastic lover and connoisseur in music," was intimate with Schubert at the Seminary and for sometime afterwards. He played second violin, later cello, in the Seminary orchestra, and describes the activity of the group as follows:

> year in and year out, at our daily performances all the [published] symphonies by Josef Haydn and Mozart, the first two symphonies by Beethoven, as well as all the Overtures we could tackle at that time, even "Coriolan" and "Leonore" (the grand Overture to Fidelio), were regularly performed . . .[4]

Schubert's principal orchestral activities after he left the Seminary have been described by Leopold von Sonnleithner (1797–1873) in the latter's extensive memoirs on domestic music-making in Vienna during the early 19th century.[5] Sonnleithner describes the origins of an amateur orchestra in the home of Schubert's father (1814); the group's constant search for larger quarters; and lists the personnel involved. Schubert appears as a violist. Sonnleithner reports that by 1818, the year in which the group dissolved, they "had become such a good ensemble that they were also able to give effective performances of the larger symphonies of Haydn, Mozart, Krommer, A. Romberg, etc. and the first two of Beethoven . . ."[6]

Op. 29, and the D minor ("Death and the Maiden"). The intended one may have been the very last of his quartets, the G major, Op. 161 (1826).—According to Deutsch, by "grand symphony" Schubert "did not mean a particular work, but the type of composition he wished to cultivate as distinct from his youthful works of this species . . ." (*SR*, p. 340).

4. *S:MF*, p. 58.

5. It was Sonnleithner who initiated the project to publish Schubert's songs by subscription. Together with Josef Hüttenbrenner, Johann Schönauer, and Johann N. Schönpichler, Sonnleithner caused ten books of Schubert's songs to appear, Opp. 1–10, 12–14. His memoirs appeared in the periodical *Rezensionen und Mitteilungen über Theater und Musik*, 1861–63.

6. Originally published in 1862. Citation from *S:MF*, p. 339.

In the same valuable collection of memoirs there are several reports concerning Schubert's favorite works. Anselm Hüttenbrenner lists a number of vocal compositions and a single orchestral work—Beethoven's Fifth Symphony.[7] A second listing comes from Josef von Spaun (1788–1865), who was one of Schubert's truest friends and, according to Deutsch, a most reliable source of information. He was leader of the second violins in the Seminary orchestra and observed with amazement the young boy's impeccable musicianship. Concerning Schubert's reaction to orchestral works, he wrote:

> The Adagios from the Haydn symphonies moved him profoundly and of the G minor Symphony [K.550] by Mozart he often said to me that it produced in him a violent emotion without his knowing exactly why. . . . With Beethoven's Symphonies in D major and A [*recte* B♭] major his delight reached its climax. Later on he liked the C minor Symphony even better.[8]

In view of Schubert's interest in cyclicism (see below, p. 109 f.),[9] it is important to observe that the Fifth is Beethoven's only cyclic symphony preceding the Ninth. Furthermore, in the Ninth themes from the first three movements are merely recalled momentarily in the finale. Derivations from the famous motif opening the Fifth, on the other hand, may be traced in each of the other movements. It is highly significant that during Schubert's own lifetime the versatile E. T. A. Hoffmann published an analysis of the Fifth in which he described the cyclic elements in detail and praised highly the principle of thematic derivation. The article was published in the important and widely read *Allgemeine Musikalische Zeitung*, Leipzig, July 4 and 11, 1810. Hoffmann, whose essays have been credited with inaugurating a new era in music criticism,

---

7. *S:MF*, p. 70.

8. *S:MF*, p. 126. Schubert's Fifth Symphony, in B♭ (1816), is his work most under the influence of Mozart's G minor Symphony. The Beethoven symphonies mentioned are the Second, in D, and, according to Deutsch, the Fourth, in B♭, rather than the Seventh, in A. The C minor is, of course, the Fifth.

9. A composition is designated as cyclic when the same or clearly related thematic materials appear in two or more relatively independent sections or movements of an extended composition. See also *Harvard Dictionary of Music,* article entitled *cyclic, cyclical,* section (2). Using the term somewhat more broadly than do many writers, the present editor designates compositions by Schubert as cyclic if thematic materials from separate movements are demonstrably derived one from another even though the resultant themes do not betray an immediate resemblance. Justification for this view rests in the fact that in both instances Schubert's intent is identical: he is concerned with strengthening the sense of over-all unity by means of thematic relationships.

was extremely well thought of by musicians of his day, including Weber and Beethoven himself.

In 1813 Hoffmann published his essay *Beethoven's Instrumental Music,* incorporating elements from the earlier study on the Fifth and from one concerning the Piano Trios, Op. 70. He particularly argued for "the deep inner coherence [*Zusammenhang*] of each composition by Beethoven." First published anonymously in the *Zeitung für die elegante Welt,* Leipzig, December 9, 10, and 11, 1813, *Beethoven's Instrumental Music* was incorporated as *Kreisleriana* No. 4 in Hoffmann's brilliantly successful collection *Fantasy Pieces in Callot's Manner,* Bamberg, 1814. There were numerous contemporary reviews of this work, a second edition in 1819, and a third in 1825. Indeed, for a number of years Hoffmann's literary fame appears to have rested on this, his first book, and each new literary publication by Hoffmann from the years 1814 to 1819 described him as the "author of the *Fantasy Pieces in Callot's Manner.*" Beethoven's conversation books indicate that he became familiar with the *Fantasy Pieces* during February or March, 1820. Almost immediately the composer—usually unapproachable—wrote an extremely friendly letter to Hoffmann, implying approval of Hoffmann's analysis of his music.[10]

With particular regard to the *Unfinished,* it is possible that Schubert was influenced by such features of the Fifth as the relating of separate movements by thematic means, the choice of the minor mode, the use of trombones,[11] and—perhaps most significantly—the dramatic power and broad scope of the development section in the first movement. The importance and explosive effectiveness of the development section of the *Unfinished* is not paralleled in Schubert's earlier symphonies or, for that matter, in his entire instrumental output.

There is, however, another symphony by Beethoven reported by von Spaun to have been one of Schubert's favorites, the Second. Thoroughly familiar with the work because of his participation in performances during his early—and most impressionable—years, Schubert seems to have absorbed much from the inner movements. This is perhaps most apparent in the slow movement and fragmentary scherzo of the *Unfinished.* Of all Beethoven's slow movements, that of the Second most suggests Schubert

---

10. The letter was published in 1823, the year after Hoffmann's death, by Eduard Hitzig in his important work *Aus Hoffmann's Leben und Nachlass.* It is quite possible, therefore, that Schubert knew of Beethoven's tacit approval of Hoffmann's analysis by way of the book, if he had not already heard of the letter earlier from a member of the Beethoven circle.

11. See p. 47, footnote 3.

and specifically the Andante con moto of the *Unfinished*. Beside the resemblances in the general spirit of the movements, including the lyricism common to both, several of Beethoven's themes could easily be mistaken for products of Schubert. Other details are similar as well. There is in the Beethoven, as in the Schubert, a graceful, somewhat nostalgic character giving way to powerful tutti passages in the subordinate section, the second group of the exposition. Although Beethoven's tempo is a bit slower, both movements are moderately rather than extremely slow. There are identical meters $(\frac{3}{8})$, related keys (Beethoven's in A, Schubert's in E), and some important rhythmic features in common. Both movements begin with primary themes that are essentially downbeat in character. The over-all rhythmic flow is similar, stressing eighth-note motion at the outset and gradually adding sixteenths and later some passages with thirty-second notes.

Certain more specific details of rhythm and orchestration are also comparable. Note the syncopated accompaniment on repeated octaves in Beethoven's violins (mm. 12–16) and in the repetition of this passage (mm. 25–32). Note especially the rhythm in m. 14, and compare it with Schubert's accompaniment for the second group played by the first violins.

Ex. 1   a) Beethoven: Larghetto, mm. 12–16

b) Schubert: Andante con moto, mm. 68–72

Other syncopations are similar in the structurally analogous passages shown in Ex. 2. Note that the syncopated lines are played first by violins alone and then doubled by flutes; that each functions as a rhythmically activated counterpoint to a primary melodic idea presented chordally; that both sections are essentially strong dynamically and follow a soft passage; and that Schubert's contrapuntal line in thirty-second notes (second violins, violas, and oboes, mm. 104–10) derives its essential

Ex. 2   a) Beethoven: Larghetto, mm. 55–58

b) Schubert: Andante con moto, mm. 96–99

melodic shape from Beethoven's second violin part in m. 61 and string parts elsewhere (e.g. mm. 101 and 105; see Ex. 3). The over-all structure

Ex. 3   a) Beethoven: Larghetto, mm. 61–62

b) mm. 100–02

of the two slow movements—sonata form—is similar, although Schubert's version is abridged (i.e. without a development section) and richer in modulations.

It may also be observed that certain details of Beethoven's Larghetto must have enchanted the young Schubert as he played in the school orchestra: the unforgettable melody of the cellos and second violins (m. 82 ff.), the following chordal passage in the syncopated rhythm ♫ ♫♫, repeated in the very next measure; the version of Beethoven's first theme in minor (m. 100 ff., Ex. 3b); and especially the repeated octaves and chords with their unexpected harmonic turns in the remainder of the development.[12]

The most convincing relationship between the Second and the *Unfinished,* however, may be traced between the Trio of Beethoven's Scherzo and Schubert's analogous, though incomplete, movement. Compare the principal themes of each (Ex. 4, a and b, on p. 106).

As may be observed, the tempos and meters are the same and the rhythms almost identical. Note that measure 7 of Beethoven's Trio provides the actual melodic shape for Schubert's quarter notes. The pair of eighth notes that serve as the upbeat for Beethoven appear, modified, as three eighth notes in the 4th and 8th measures of Schubert's orchestrated fragment and frequently thereafter in his piano sketches. In both Beethoven and Schubert, the upbeats consist of brief, ascending segments of a scale; the exact figure of two eighths appears in Schubert's measures 16, 18, and 20.

As in his first movement, the principal contrast for the first part of Schubert's Scherzo is provided by a modulation to the region of the submediant, G major. This statement (Ex. 4c) provides the melodic shape that is closest to Beethoven's. As will be seen later, the theme under discussion also constitutes the most important cyclic feature for Schubert's composition.

Following the double bar and repeat signs, Schubert writes a passage in two-part imitative counterpoint, in the key of the subdominant. Both key and counterpoint are reminiscent of the analogous spot in the first movement (i.e. in the development section). Of more direct interest at the moment, however, is the fact that two-part imitation is also important for Beethoven's Scherzo and Trio. The opening of the Scherzo, for example, consists of a rising figure stated first in the bass and then in the upper parts, in alternating fashion. In fact, this textural approach dominates Beethoven's Scherzo. There is also some imitation in the last phrase of Beethoven's Trio.

A point remains to be made with respect to Beethoven's orchestration. The return of the principal theme of the Trio is scored for horns with violins doubling, while the bass line consists of a descending scale, played pizzicato, for the cellos and double basses; after four measures the first bassoon doubles the horn and first violin (see Ex. 5). This should

---

12. There are numerous similar passages in Schubert's instrumental music; see, for example, the slow movement of one of his last works, the A major Piano Sonata, (D. 959), middle section.

Ex. 4   a) Beethoven: Trio, mm. 1–8

b) Schubert: 3rd mvt. (orch. version), mm. 1–8

c) 3rd mvt. (piano sketches), mm. 25–32

d) 3rd mvt. (piano sketches), Trio, mm. 1–8

e) 1st mvt., mm. 1–6

f) 1st mvt., mm. 13–17

g) 1st mvt., mm. 184–87

h) 2nd mvt., mm. 3–7

i) 2nd mvt., mm. 18–22

j) 2nd mvt., mm. 33–40

be compared with the first three measures of Schubert's Andante con moto. Notice that, in addition to the scoring, the melodic and rhythmic shape of the two lines is almost identical.

Ex. 5 Beethoven: Trio, mm. 33–40

Although it does not directly affect the *Unfinished*, Beethoven's system of key relationships must have made a deep impression on Schubert. The principal harmonic contrast of Beethoven's D major Scherzo is provided by the key of the lowered submediant, B♭ (mm. 19–29). In the final section the area of the lowered mediant, F major, is emphasized twice (mm. 56–60 and 67–68). As is well known, passages stressing chromatically altered mediant or submediant regions are characteristic of

Schubert's music, particularly in compositions whose mode is major.

Was Schubert consciously attempting to emulate Beethoven's Second? I do not believe so. For one thing, there are no cyclic aspects in Beethoven's symphony and there is much evidence to indicate that cyclicism was on Schubert's mind at this time. His very next composition was the *Wanderer Fantasy,* Op. 15, written in the following month, November of 1822, and a work in which cyclicism is of the utmost importance.

Furthermore, there are cyclic elements in each of the next four chamber works he wrote, all dating from 1824.[13] A fifth larger instrumental work, the *Divertissement à la hongroise* for piano duet, dates from the same year and is also cyclic. As Schubert noted in the letter to Kupelwieser, three of the four chamber compositions were expressly written to pave his way towards "grand symphony." [14]

Finally, the thematic similarities to the Beethoven are much too close for comfort. In this respect, Johann Leopold Ebner's story concerning Schubert's song *Die Forelle (The Trout)* and Beethoven's *Coriolan* Overture is significant. Ebner (1791–1870), like von Spaun, was a fellow student in the orchestra. His many copies of Schubert's songs were an important source for the *Gesamtausgabe*. On May 3, 1858, he wrote:

> After Schubert had composed the song, "Die Forelle," he brought it the same day to us in the Seminary to try over and it was repeated several times with the most lively pleasure; suddenly Holzapfel cried: "Good Heavens, Schubert, you got that out of 'Coriolan.' "
>
> In the Overture to that opera [*sic*] [15] there is, in fact, a passage which bears a resemblance to the pianoforte accompaniment in the "Forelle"; Schubert saw this at once, too, and wanted to destroy the song, but we would not allow it and thus saved that glorious song from destruction.[16]

Ebner later confirmed the story in a letter dated June 4, 1858: "the story that he [Schubert] wished to destroy it [the song *Die Forelle*] is literally true and moreover *I was there at the time.*" [17]

13. See Martin Chusid, *Schubert's Cyclic Compositions of 1824,* in *Acta Musicologica,* XXXVI (1964), 37–45.

14. See p. 99 above.

15. Beethoven's Overture to *Coriolanus* was written for a play by Heinrich von Collin, not for an opera.

16. *S:MF,* p. 47.

17. *S:MF,* p. 49; the italics are Ebner's. In addition to Holzapfel, another witness to the event, Albert Stadler, was named in this letter. Both Holzapfel and Stadler were alive when Ebner's story was made public and could easily have denied it if it were false.—The point of resemblance is actually small, primarily the use, in the accompaniment to the text "So zückte seine Ruhe," of a dotted rhythm that also

Here lies a possible answer to the most puzzling of all questions concerning the *Unfinished:* why did Schubert break off so abruptly in the course of writing his B minor Symphony? The answer may be that while working on the final, orchestral version of the third movement he became consciously aware of the thematic relationship with Beethoven's Trio. One may well ask at this point why he did not simply replace the Scherzo with another. For the answer to that, we must examine the extent of Schubert's use of related themes in the *Unfinished* (see Ex. 4 above).

The themes cited reveal a remarkable consistency of melodic approach. Note especially the bracketed figure of three short notes followed by a longer one to be found in each. In every instance this figure is preceded by notes of longer note value, most often two in number. There are other aspects in common:

a) All the movements, and consequently the themes, are in triple meter.
b) All the themes begin on the downbeat.
c) The themes are uniformly melodic—that is, they are conceived in melodic phrases of at least four measures in length, rather than as successions suggesting concise, independent motifs.
d) Almost all of the melodic phrases fall within a narrow range, usually no more than a sixth.
e) Intervals of a second or third predominate melodically. Frequently the interval of the third is filled in, either immediately before or after being sounded.

While certain of these resemblances may be coincidental, it is not likely that all of them were. The evidence offered by the *Wanderer Fantasy* and the cyclic compositions of 1824 further strengthens the hypothesis that Schubert was intentionally seeking to unify the individual movements of the *Unfinished* by melodic means. With the sole exception of the downbeat beginning, it may be noted that the theme of Beethoven's Trio contains all of the unifying features mentioned above.[18]

---

plays an important part in the Overture (see, for example, m. 260 ff.). The story does, however, illustrate Schubert's extreme sensitivity to the suggestion of plagiarism. In this respect it may be observed that, contrary to 18th-century custom, plagiarism was increasingly frowned upon in the early 19th century. Witness the many copyright laws of the time and the comment by the contemporary English essayist William Hazlitt (1778–1830), who wrote, "If an author is once detected in borrowing he will be suspected of plagiarism ever after." (Cited from *The Oxford Universal Dictionary on Historical Principles,* 3rd rev. ed. with addenda, Oxford, 1955, p. 1513.)

18. Beethoven transfers the upbeat from the melody to the bass to begin the restatement of the opening theme during the second part of the Trio. This was the same passage whose orchestration anticipated the opening of Schubert's Andante con moto (see Ex. 5, p. 107 above).

Now, perhaps, we can understand Schubert's dilemma. He could not remove the offending themes—those resembling Beethoven's Trio—without destroying the completed movements as well as the fragmentary Scherzo. The problem was seemingly insoluble and he felt compelled to abandon the composition.

The theory advanced above rests on three basic premises: first, that Schubert was concerned at this stage of his compositional career with unifying his symphonies cyclicly; secondly, that the movements of the *Unfinished* are so unified; and finally, that he would be disturbed by the charge of thematic plagiarism.

In the opening essay it was argued that Schubert ceased work on the *Unfinished* because of a compositional problem and not in response to a non-musical, external pressure.[19] The hypothesis advanced here suggests the exact nature of that problem and at the same time justifies the interruption and failure to complete the work. It also suggests a reason for Schubert's complete silence concerning the symphony in subsequent years, years during which he was more concerned than ever before with large-scale instrumental works, many of them magnificent compositions with a strong claim to our attention and affection. None, however, surpasses—and few approach—in quality or dramatic effect the completed movements of the *Unfinished Symphony.*

19. See p. 9 above.

VIEWS
AND COMMENTS

EDUARD HANSLICK

[*On the First Performance*] †

The first performance of the *Unfinished* took place at noon on Sunday, December 17, 1865, in the Grosser Redoutensaal of the Imperial Palace in Vienna.

Eduard Hanslick (1825–1904) was probably the leading Austrian writer on esthetics and music history during the 19th century. A lecturer and later professor at the University of Vienna, he also wrote music criticism for several Viennese newspapers. Hanslick was a staunch supporter of the music of Schumann and Brahms but opposed the esthetic premises underlying program music (e.g. the symphonic poems of Liszt) as well as the music-dramas of Wagner. In retaliation, Wagner caricatured Hanslick as the pedantic Beckmesser, in his opera *Die Meistersinger von Nürnberg* (first performed in Munich, 1868).

Among the so-called "Friends of Schubert" *par excellence,* two characteristic groups stand out: the indifferent and the stubborn, or expressed in physical terms, the centrifugals and the centripetals. Members of the first group serenely allow Schubert's manuscripts to be scattered to the four corners of the earth; they know, or they knew, the details of one or another opera or symphony still extant (indeed, they saw it originate!), but it does not disturb their peace of mind in the least if these treasures fall to an American collector for a few gulden or still cheaper to a cheesemonger. The misers or centripetals, on the other hand, have two or three pearls from Schubert's legacy carefully hidden away, locked up somewhere in a chest whose key they take to bed. Yet they profess nothing but friendship for the immortalized one and nothing but disdain for the living. As of yesterday we shall no longer count Anselm Hüttenbrenner as a member of the second class, since he finally succumbed to the persuasive loquacity of the Court Music Director Herbeck. The latter expressly set out for Graz in order to obtain a score by Hüttenbrenner for the Society Orchestral Concerts [1] and at the same time—how strange—

† From Hanslick, *Geschichte des Concertwesens in Wien, Aus dem Concertsaal,* Vienna, 1870, II, 350–51. Translation by the editor.

1. Concerts sponsored by the Gesellschaft der Musikfreunde (Society for the

also brought back a long-sought manuscript by Schubert. We cannot
decide which of the two compositions was the bait and which the fish;
suffice it to say that Schubert and Hüttenbrenner, as in life, were har-
moniously united on the program of the last Society concert. Hüttenbrenner, who as is well known contributed much to the fame of Schubert's *Erlkönig,* namely a group of "Erlkönig waltzes," opened the concert with an Overture in C minor to which one cannot deny a certain
solidity and formal competence. Then there followed the Schubert novelty, which excited an extraordinary amount of enthusiasm. It consisted
of the first two movements (Allegro moderato, B minor, and Andante
[con moto], E major) of a symphony that was presumed to be lost but
was, in fact, in Herr Hüttenbrenner's possession for forty years. The
score in question, completely in Schubert's hand, bears the date 1822 and,
in addition to the first two movements, also contains the beginning of
a third, nine measures of a Scherzo in B minor.[2] Whether Schubert worked
further on the composition cannot be determined. Possibly a member of
the indifferent group is capable of solving the riddle, or perhaps one of
the stubborn has the solution under his pillow. We must rest content
with the two movements which, awakened to new life by Herbeck, have
also brought new life into our concert halls. When, after the few introductory measures, clarinets and oboes in unison begin to sound their
sweet song above the peaceful murmur of the violins, then each and every
child recognizes the composer, and a half-suppressed outcry "Schubert"
buzzes through the hall. He has hardly entered, but it is as if one knows
him by his step, by his manner of lifting the latch. After that yearning
song in minor, there now sounds in the cellos a contrasting theme in G
major, an enchanting passage of song of almost *Ländler*-like ease.[3] Then
every heart rejoices, as if Schubert were standing alive in our midst after
a long separation. The entire movement is a sweet stream of melody;
despite the power and originality so crystal clear that one can see every
pebble on the bottom. And everywhere the same warmth, the same golden,

---

Friends of Music), an organization founded in 1812 and still active today. Their
valuable archives contain the autograph manuscripts of all the completed symphonies by Schubert except the Fifth. [*Editor*]

 2. Apparently Hanslick was not aware at that time of the extensive piano sketches
for the third movement or the second page of score. [*Editor*]

 3. A *Ländler* is a folk or folk-like dance in a slow or moderate triple meter. Dances
of this character have been widespread in South Germany and Austria for centuries,
although the term *Ländler* itself seems to be of relatively recent origin (c. 1800), as
is indicated by Felix Hoerburger in *Die Musik in Geschichte und Gegenwart,* VIII
(1960), 55. See also *Grove's Dictionary* and the *Harvard Dictionary of Music.* [*Editor*]

life-giving sunshine. The Andante unfolds itself more broadly and at greater length. It is a song full of fervor and quiet happiness, where tones of lament or anger fall only here and there suggesting more the effect of musical thunderclouds than the dangerous passion of violent emotion. As if he could not separate himself from his own sweet song, the composer postpones the conclusion of the Adagio [*sic*], yes, postpones it all too long. One knows this characteristic of Schubert, a trait that weakens the total effect of many of his compositions. At the close of the Andante his flight seems to lose itself beyond the reach of the eye, nevertheless one may still hear the rustling of his wings.

The beauty of sonority in both movements is bewitching. With a few horn passages, here and there a short clarinet or oboe solo on the simplest, most natural orchestral base, Schubert gains effects of sonority that no craftiness of Wagnerian instrumentation achieves. We number the newly found symphonic fragment of Schubert among his most beautiful instrumental works, and do so the more cheerfully since on more than one occasion we have allowed ourselves a word of warning against an overly zealous Schubert idolatry.

SIR GEORGE GROVE

[*A Trip to Vienna*] †

Sir George Grove (1820–1900) was the first editor for the *Dictionary of Music and Musicians* that still bears his name. Although an engineer by profession, he participated actively in other areas and was secretary for the Society of Arts. After the Exhibition of 1851 he became secretary of the Crystal Palace and from 1856 to 1896 wrote analytical program notes for their concerts. He was, finally, the first Principal of the newly founded Royal College of Music (1882–94). Without a doubt Grove was the most influential champion of Schubert's music in England during the 19th century and, despite the fact that he was not trained as a professional musician, his writings radiate a warmth and enthusiasm still contagious today.

† From the Appendix on Schubert's symphonies in the English edition of Heinrich Kreissle von Hellborn, *The Life of Franz Schubert*, London, 1869, pp. 297–301.

On the 5th October, 1867, I had the happiness to find myself for the first time in the city of Vienna. It was a place which I had looked forward to, almost hopelessly, as a kind of El Dorado, for years. I was with one of my best friends, and the object of my visit was as dear and congenial to me as possible. Could I have been more happily situated?

My immediate object was to endeavour to obtain some of the great orchestral works of Franz Schubert, which I had reason to believe were lying neglected, or at least unperformed, there; and of these especially his Symphonies, and the completion of the incidental music to the Drama of 'Rosamunde.'

My readers must know that I am Secretary to the Crystal Palace Company, that I take a lively personal (as well as official and commercial) interest in the success of the 'Saturday Concerts,' and that it was mainly in relation to these that my enthusiasm for Franz Schubert had arisen, and had led me to Vienna.

My acquaintance with the music of this truly remarkable composer began in the year 1846 or 1847, and was then confined to his songs, of which, however, I knew not only those commonly known, but others, then more rarely tried; not only the 'Müllerlieder,' the 'Erlkönig,' and the 'Wanderer,' but the series of the 'Winterreise' and the 'Schwanengesang,' as well as such detached songs as 'Todesmusik,' the 'Lied der Anna Lyle,' 'An eine Quelle,' and a few other less-known songs.

Thus it remained till 1856 or 1857, in which year, with very inadequate means, Mr. Manns, the admirable conductor of the Crystal Palace orchestra, and my very kind and excellent friend, played the C major Symphony of Schubert, the only one of his orchestral works then known in England; at that time, too, believed to be his only Symphony, and, if I am right, never before played in England, though since performed by the Musical Society of London, and by the 'New Philharmonic Society' of Dr. Wylde. Mr. Manns's band had also Schubert's 'Overture to Rosamunde' (Op. 26) in their repertoire. The C major Symphony was performed at the Crystal Palace more than once during the following years; but the band was then so small, and the locality so unfavourable, and the Symphony itself so long for ordinary ears, that it is not wonderful it should have achieved no success, and awakened no enthusiasm.

This went on till the year 1865, when the 'Life of Schubert,' by Dr. Kreissle von Hellborn, of which the present work is a translation, was published. It at once attracted my attention; I was delighted with the catalogue at the end, and especially interested with the *entr'actes* to the drama of 'Rosamunde,' which were therein described. I at once corresponded with Mr. Spina, the well-known music-publisher of Vienna, successor to the ancient firm of Diabelli & Co., with whom the Crystal Palace Company had already had communications on matters of business. Mr. Spina met my advances in the most gratifying way. He informed me that the parts of several numbers of the 'Rosamunde' music were in his possession, and that two of them were then in the press. These were the *entr'actes* between the first and second, and third and fourth acts, in B minor and B-flat respectively. The printed score and parts of these arrived at the end of October, 1866; they were immediately tried, and great was our delight to find how original and beautiful they were. They were first played on this side the water on the 10th November, 1866, with the lovely Romance in F minor, sung by Mdlle. Enequist, and scored for this occasion by Mr. Manns from the pianoforte arrangement in which it was published by Schubert. They were most favourably received, and have become stock-pieces in the repertory of the Crystal Palace music. This success naturally increased our appetite for more of the same treasures, and after some correspondence, we obtained two more numbers of the same composition—this time in MS. The first of these, 'No 2, Ballo,' is a piece in the fashion of an *entr'acte,* in the key of B minor, like No. 1, and to a certain extent formed on the same themes, though with different treatment, and ending in a most naïve and charming curtain-tune in G major. The other, No. 9, is a Ballet Air, also in G, and in Schubert's best and liveliest style. This was first played on the 16th March, 1867.

But the 'Rosamunde' music was not, even as far as we then knew it, complete. The three Choruses had, like the Romance, been printed during Schubert's lifetime with pianoforte accompaniment; the trombone parts to the 'Geister-Chor' were also printed. But all enquiries for the orchestral accompaniments to the other two, or to the Romance, failed to produce any result. Mr. Spina had not got them, and could not tell who had.

In the course of the autumn we received from Mr. Spina MS. copies of the Overtures to 'Alfonso and Estrella' and 'Fierrabras,' which were performed at the concerts of November 3rd, 1866, and February 2nd, 1867, respectively. The latter of these was not entirely new to England, having been brought over by Mendelssohn with the MS. of the great C major Symphony, No. 9, and played at the Philharmonic under his direction on June 10, 1864; but it does not appear to have been repeated, and the Overture to 'Alfonso and Estrella' had certainly never been played in this country. A little later we received from our good correspondent in Vienna the score and parts of the 'Overture in the Italian Style in C,' since published as Op. 170, which was also an entire novelty, and was first played on December 1, 1866. These works are all characteristic and interesting, but they were thrown into the shade by the unfinished Symphony in B minor, No. 8, which was published early in 1867, and which we received on April 2, and first performed at the concert of the following Saturday, April 6, 1867.

This most original and beautiful composition stimulated our desire to obtain more of the same kind of music in the very highest degree. I eagerly asked everyone whom I met—Mr. Joachim, Madame Schumann, and others—for information as to the rest of the Symphonies, but without success; no one had seen them or knew anything about them. At length, in the autumn of '68,[1] a succession of fortunate circumstances, for which I can never be too grateful, put it into my power to visit Vienna, in company with a gentleman who is at once one of my best friends, and—in the absence of Mr. Manns, then unable to leave his duties—better able, perhaps, than anyone else to advise and assist me in my search, namely, Mr. Arthur Sullivan.[2]

At Vienna, then, we arrived on October the 5th, and our first care was to make the acquaintance of Dr. Schneider. This we were enabled to do through the kindness and tact of Mr. Spina, who proved himself in every way a valuable friend. Dr. Schneider's office, or chambers (for he is a barrister in full practice) is in the Tuchlauben. First, there is the spacious outer room, or clerks' office; then, behind it, Dr. Schneider's own sanctum, and in a roomy cupboard in this are contained the treasures which we had come to seek. We had sent our letters of introduction before us, and on calling found the doctor ready to receive us, with the books on the table before him. A quarter of an hour's conversation was sufficient to put us perfectly *en rapport,* and I soon had the scores of the first, second, third, fourth, and sixth of Schubert's Symphonies in my hands.

Two things strike one in a Schubert manuscript—its remarkable neatness and freedom from erasures or corrections, and the careful man-

1. This is either a memory lapse or a slip of the pen. Grove's trip took place in the autumn of 1867. [*Editor*]

2. Sir Arthur S. Sullivan (1842–1900), English composer and Professor of Composition at the Royal Academy of Music, later became famous for his operettas, particularly those on librettos by W. S. Gilbert. [*Editor*]

ner in which it is dated and signed. The signature always has *mpia.,* i.e. 'manu propriâ,' after it. Often the separate movements are dated; and we shall find one instance of the hour and minute of the beginning and ending of a movement having been recorded.

I took my treasures to a table by the window in the clerks' office, and worked quietly at them till I had got all that I was able.***

The Eighth Symphony: in B minor †

This, like the preceding,[1] is unfinished, but in a different manner. The two first movements are complete, and nine bars of the third; but there the composition absolutely stops: no hint remains to guide us to the remainder.[2] At the time of our visit to Vienna, the MS. was in the hands of Mr. Herbeck, who was kind enough to show it to us. It is on oblong paper, very freely but very neatly written, with great grace in the writing, and with very rare corrections. On the first page is the date, 'Wien, d. 30te Oct. 1822.'

The score and parts are published, and the Symphony is performed so frequently at the Crystal Palace [3] and elsewhere, and has been so often commented upon, that it is unnecessary for me to say anything of its many and remarkable beauties, except that (speaking as a mere amateur) every time I hear it I am confirmed in the belief that it stands quite apart from all other compositions of Schubert or any other master. It must be the record of some period of unusual *attendrissement* and depression, unusual even for the susceptible and passionate nature of Schubert.

What a commentary do these two movements form on the following sentence from his Journal!—'My compositions are the result of my abili-

---

† From the English edition of Hellborn's biography, pp. 317–18.
1. Grove is referring to the Symphonic Sketch in E, D. 729, dating from early August 1821. [*Editor*]
2. It is clear that at this time Grove knew nothing of the piano sketches. [*Editor*]
3. The score was published early in 1867, and the Symphony was first performed at the Crystal Palace on the 6th April. It was also played by the Philharmonic Society on the 20th May in the same year.

ties and my distress; and those which distress alone has engendered appear to give the world most pleasure.' [4]

This and No. 5 are the only ones out of the nine which have no Introduction to the first movement.

HUGO WOLF

[*On the Unfinished Symphony*] †

The Austrian composer Hugo Wolf (1860–1903) was music critic for the weekly *Wiener Salonblatt* from 1883 to 1887. Although he wrote instrumental works and even opera, it was "in his songs, in which he attained the highest."

The B minor Symphony, a true reflection of the artistic individuality of its creator, was unfortunately left a fragment. So it compares in its form with the external existence of the master, who in the flower of his life, at the height of his creative powers, was snatched away by Death. Schubert lived only half a lifetime, as a man and also as an artist. His life barely sufficed for him to write two symphonic movements consummate in content and form. We possess to be sure a precious legacy from him in the C major Symphony, but all the flowering riches of his ideas, the voluptuous spell of his melodies, cannot hide from us the loose construction of its symphonic architecture. The B minor Symphony is not only more compact, more formally unified than the C major, in its themes the pathetic Schubert speaks as convincingly as the dreamily elegiac. He reveals himself as completely as in his songs, in which he attained the highest.

4. From Schubert's lost notebook of 1824. See *SR*, p. 336. [*Editor*]
† Translation from Frank Walker, *Hugo Wolf: A Biography*, London, 1951, pp. 150–51.

ANTONÍN DVOŘÁK

[Schubert's Music] †

The Bohemian composer Antonín Dvořák (1841–1904) was artistic director of the National Conservatory in New York from 1892 to 1895. This article, one of the earliest serious studies of Schubert's music to be published in America, appeared shortly after the world première by the New York Philharmonic of Dvořák's Symphony *From The New World* (Dec. 13, 1893). His remarks about Schubert's influence on Romantic composers, including himself, are of especial interest.

Surprise has often been expressed that the Viennese (among whom he lived) and the publishers should not have appreciated him more substantially; yet it is not difficult to find reasons for this in the circumstances of the case. While a pianist or singer may find immediate recognition, a composer, especially if he has so original a message to deliver as Schubert, has to bide his time. We must bear in mind how very young he was when he died. Dr. Hanslick has urged, in defense of the Viennese, that only seven years elapsed between the publication of Schubert's first works and his death, and that during his lifetime he became known chiefly as a song composer; and songs were at that time not sung at public concerts, but only in the domestic circle. Moreover, Rossini on the one hand, and Beethoven on the other, overshadowed the modest young Schubert.*** As regards Schubert's orchestral works, we must remember that orchestras were not at that time what they are to-day. The best Viennese organization, the Gesellschaft der Musikfreunde, found the symphony in C "too long and too difficult" at the rehearsal, and substituted an earlier work. This was in 1828, the year of the composer's death. Ten years later the zealous Schumann discovered the great symphony in C and took it to Leipsic, where the equally enthusiastic Mendelssohn secured for it a noteworthy success. In Vienna, too, it was taken up again in the following

† From the article *Franz Schubert,* in *The Century Magazine,* XLVIII (July 1894), 341–48, written by Dvořák in cooperation with Henry T. Finck.

year, but only two movements were given, and these were separated by a Donizetti aria! Three years later Habeneck attempted to produce this symphony in Paris, but the band rebelled over the first movement, and the same result followed in London, two years later still, when Mendelssohn put it in rehearsal for a Philharmonic concert. These things seem strange to us, but they are historic fact, and help to explain why Schubert, with all his melody and spontaneity, made his way so slowly to popular appreciation. He was young, modest, and unknown, and musicians did not hesitate to slight a symphony which they would have felt bound to study, had it borne the name of Beethoven or Mozart.

But his fame has grown steadily from year to year, and will grow greater still in the next century. Rubinstein [1] has, perhaps, gone farther than any one, not only in including Schubert in the list of those he considers the five greatest composers,—Bach, Beethoven, Schubert, Chopin, Glinka—but in exclaiming, "Once more, and a thousand times more, Bach, Beethoven, and Schubert are the highest summits in music" ("Die Musik und Ihre Meister," p. 50) . I am asked whether I approve of this classification. Such questions are difficult to answer. I should follow Rubinstein in including Schubert in the list of the very greatest composers, but I should not follow him in omitting Mozart. Schubert and Mozart have much in common; in both we find the same delicate sense of instrumental coloring, the same spontaneous and irrepressible flow of melody, the same instinctive command of the means of expression, and the same versatility in all the branches of their art. In their amazing fertility, too, they were alike.

* * *

Schubert contributed to every form of his art; he was, as I have said, as versatile as Mozart, to whom he bears so many points of resemblance. But in one respect these two masters differ widely. Mozart was greatest in the opera, where Schubert was weakest. Schubert's attempts to exercise his genius and improve his fortunes by writing operas came at an unpropitious moment—a time when Vienna was so Rossini-mad that even Beethoven was discouraged from writing for the stage. It took several rebuffs to discourage Schubert; indeed, though all his attempts failed, he is said to have had further operatic projects at the time of his last illness. He was always unlucky with his librettos, which are, without exception, inadequate. There were other untoward circumstances; yet the chief cause of his failure lay, after all, in the nature of his genius, which was

1. Anton Rubinstein (1829–94) , famous Russian pianist and composer. [*Editor*]

lyrical, and not dramatic, or, at any rate, not theatrical. When Liszt produced "Alfonso und Estrella" at Weimar in 1854, it had only a *succès d'estime,* and Liszt himself confessed that its performance must be regarded merely as *ein Akt der Pietät,* and an execution of historic justice. He called attention to the strange fact that Schubert, who in his songs contributed such picturesque and expressive accompaniments, should in this opera have assigned to the instruments such a subordinate rôle that it seemed little more than a pianoforte accompaniment arranged for the orchestra. At the same time, as Liszt very properly adds, Schubert influenced the progress of opera *indirectly,* by showing in his *songs* how closely poetry can be wedded to music, and that it can be emotionally intensified by its impassioned accents. Nor must we overlook the fact that there are in these Schubert operas not a few melodies, beautiful as such, which we can enjoy at home or in the concert hall. These melodies were too lyrical in style to save the operas; they lacked also the ornamental brilliancy and theatrical dash which enabled Rossini to succeed temporarily with poor librettos, and with a less genuine dramatic instinct than Schubert has shown in some of his songs, such as the "Erl King" and especially the "Doppelgänger," where we come across chords and modulations that affect us like the weird harmonies of *Ortrud's* scenes in "Lohengrin."

*   *   *

Schubert's chamber music, especially his string quartets and his trios for pianoforte, violin, and violoncello, must be ranked among the very best of their kind in all musical literature. Of the quartets, the one in D minor is, in my opinion, the most original and important, the one in A minor the most fascinating. Schubert does not try to give his chamber music an orchestral character, yet he attains a marvelous variety of beautiful tonal effects. Here, as elsewhere, his flow of melody is spontaneous, incessant, and irrepressible, leading often to excessive diffuseness. Like Chopin and Rossini, Schubert has frequently shown how a melody may be created which can wonderfully charm us even apart from the harmonic accompaniment which naturally goes with and enriches it. But he was accused by his contemporaries of neglecting polyphony, or the art of interweaving several melodious parts into a contrapuntal web. This charge, combined with a late study of Handel's scores, induced him shortly before his death to plan a course in counterpoint with Sechter. No doubt his education in counterpoint had been neglected.[2] It is not likely, how-

2. Dvořák appears not to have known that Schubert studied counterpoint as well

ever, that such study would have materially altered his style. That was too individual from the beginning to undergo much change, for Schubert did not outgrow his early style so noticeably as did Beethoven and Wagner, for example. Besides, Schubert had no real need of contrapuntal study. In his chamber music, as in his symphonies, we often find beautiful specimens of polyphonic writing,—see, for instance, the andantes of the C major quintet and of the D minor quartet,—and though his polyphony be different from Bach's or Beethoven's, it is none the less admirable. Mendelssohn is undoubtedly a greater master of polyphony than Schubert, yet I prefer Schubert's chamber music to Mendelssohn's.

Of Schubert's symphonies, too, I am such an enthusiastic admirer that I do not hesitate to place him next to Beethoven, far above Mendelssohn, as well as above Schumann. Mendelssohn had some of Mozart's natural instinct for orchestration and gift for form, but much of his work has proved ephemeral. Schumann is at his best in his songs, his chamber music, and his pianoforte pieces. His symphonies, too, are great works, yet they are not always truly orchestral; the form seems to hamper the composer, and the instrumentation is not always satisfactory. This is never the case with Schubert. Although he sometimes wrote carelessly, and often too diffusely, he is never at fault in his means of expression, while mastery of form came to him spontaneously. In originality of harmony and modulation, and in his gift of orchestral coloring, Schubert has had no superior. Dr. Riemann [3] asserts with justice that in their use of harmony both Schumann and Liszt are descendants of Schubert; Brahms, too, whose enthusiasm for Schubert is well known, has perhaps felt his influence; and as for myself, I cordially acknowledge my great obligations to him.

I have just observed that mastery of form came to Schubert spontaneously. This is illustrated by his early symphonies, five of which he wrote before he was twenty, at which, the more I study them, the more I marvel. Although the influence of Haydn and Mozart is apparent in them, Schubert's musical individuality is unmistakable in the character of the melody, in the harmonic progressions, and in many exquisite bits of orchestration. In his later symphonies he becomes more and more in-

---

as composition with Antonio Salieri. Whether Salieri's lessons were adequate or not is a moot point. (See D. 25, three pages of unpublished contrapuntal exercises. On the first page is the statement: "Counterpoint begun June 18, 1812.") [*Editor*]

    3. Hugo Riemann (1849–1919), a celebrated German music historian and theorist. [*Editor*]

dividual and original. The influence of Haydn and Mozart, so obvious in his earlier efforts, is gradually eliminated, and with his contemporary, Beethoven, he had less in common from the beginning. He resembles Beethoven, however, in the vigor and melodious flow of his basses; such basses we find already in his early symphonies. His "Unfinished Symphony" and the great one in C are unique contributions to musical literature, absolutely new and original, Schubert in every bar. What is perhaps most characteristic about them is the song-like melody pervading them. He introduced the song into the symphony, and made the transfer so skilfully that Schumann was led to speak of the resemblance to the human voice (*Aehnlichkeit mit dem Stimmorgan*) in these orchestral parts.

Although these two symphonies are by far the best of Schubert's, it is a pity that they alone should be deemed worthy a place on our concert programs. I played the sixth in C major and No. 5 in B [flat] major a dozen times with my orchestral pupils at the National Conservatory last winter; they shared my pleasure in them, and recognized at once their great beauty.

It was with great pleasure and feelings of gratitude that I read not long ago of the performance in Berlin of the B [flat] major symphony by Herr Weingartner, one of the few conductors who have had the courage to put this youthful work on their programs. Schubert's fourth, too, is an admirable composition. It bears the title of "Tragic Symphony," and was written at the age of nineteen, about a year after the "Erl King." It makes one marvel that one so young should have had the power to give utterance to such deep pathos. In the adagio there are chords that strikingly suggest the anguish of *Tristan's* utterances; nor is this the only place wherein Schubert is prophetic of Wagnerian harmonies. And although partly anticipated by Gluck and Mozart, he was one of the first to make use of an effect to which Wagner and other modern composers owe many of their most beautiful orchestral colors—the employment of the brass, not for noise, but played softly, to secure rich and warm tints.

The richness and variety of coloring in the great symphony in C are astounding. It is a work which always fascinates, always remains new. It has the effect of gathering clouds, with constant glimpses of sunshine breaking through them. It illustrates also, like most of Schubert's compositions, the truth of an assertion once made to me by Dr. Hans Richter—that the greatest masters always reveal their genius most unmistakably and most delightfully in their slow movements. Personally, I prefer the

Unfinished Symphony even to the one in C; apart from its intrinsic beauty, it avoids the fault of diffuseness.

If Schubert's symphonies have a serious fault, it is prolixity; he does not know when to stop; yet, if the repeats are omitted, a course of which I thoroughly approve, and which, indeed, is now generally adopted, they are not too long. Schubert's case, in fact, is not an exception to, but an illustration of, the general rule that symphonies are made too long. When Bruckner's eighth symphony was produced in Vienna last winter, the Philharmonic Society had to devote a whole concert to it. The experiment has not been repeated anywhere, and there can be no doubt that this symphony would have a better chance of making its way in the world if it were shorter. This remark has a general application. We should return to the symphonic dimensions approved by Haydn and Mozart. In this respect Schumann is a model, especially in his B flat major and D minor symphonies; also in his chamber music. Modern taste calls for music that is concise, condensed, and pithy.

In Germany, England, and America, Schubert's instrumental works, chamber and orchestral, have long since enjoyed a vogue and popularity which have amply atoned for their neglect at first. As for the French, they have produced two Schubert biographies, but it cannot be said that they have shown the same general sympathy for this master as for some other German composers, or as the English have, thanks largely to the enthusiastic efforts of my esteemed friend, Sir George Grove. It is on record that after Habeneck had made an unsuccessful effort (his musicians rebelled at the rehearsal) to produce the great symphony in C at a Conservatoire concert, no further attempt was made with Schubert's orchestral compositions at these concerts for forty years.

This may help to explain the extraordinary opinion of the eminent French critic, Fétis, that Schubert is less original in his instrumental works than in his songs, the popularity of which, too, he declared to be largely a matter of fashion! The latter insinuation is of course too absurd to call for comment to-day, but as regards the first part of his criticism I do not hesitate to say that, greatly as I esteem Schubert's songs, I value his instrumental works even more highly. Were all of his compositions to be destroyed but two, I should say, save the last two symphonies.

Fortunately we are not confronted by any such necessity. The loss of Schubert's pianoforte pieces and songs would indeed be irreparable. For although much of their spirit and substance has passed into the works of his imitators and legitimate followers, the originals have never been equaled in their way. In most of his works Schubert is unique in melody, rhythm, modulation, and orchestration, but from a formal point of view he is most original in his songs and his short pieces for piano. In his symphonies, chamber music, operas, and sacred compositions, he follows classical models; but in the *Lied*, the "Musical Moment," the "Impromptu," he is romanticist in every fiber. Yet he wrote no fewer than twenty-four sonatas for pianoforte, two or four hands, in which he follows classical models, and we can trace the influence of Beethoven's style even in the three which he wrote in the last year of his life. This seems strange at first when we consider that in the *Lied* and the short pianoforte pieces he betrayed no such influence even in his earliest days. The "Erl King" and "The Wanderer," written when he was eighteen and nineteen respectively, are Schubert in every bar, whereas the piano sonatas and symphonies of this period are much more imitative, much less individual. One reason for this, doubtless, is that just as it is easier to write a short lyric poem than a long epic, so it is easier for a young composer to be original in short forms than in the more elaborate sonata and symphony; and we must remember that Schubert died at thirty-one.

But there was another reason. The tendency of the romantic school has been toward short forms, and although Weber helped to show the way, to Schubert belongs the chief credit of originating the short models of piano-forte pieces which the romantic school has preferably cultivated. His "Musical Moments" are unique, and it may be said that in the third "Impromptu" (Op. 90) lie the germs of the whole of Mendelssohn's "Songs without Words." Schumann has remarked that Schubert's style is more idiomatically pianistic (*claviermässig*) than Beethoven's, and this is perhaps true of these short pieces. Yet it can hardly be said that either Schubert or Schumann was in this respect equal to Bach or Chopin, who of all composers have written the most idiomatically for the piano. I cannot agree with Schumann in his rather depreciatory notice of Schubert's last sonatas (he speaks of "greater simplicity of invention," "a voluntary dispensing with brilliant novelty," and connects this with Schubert's last illness). I would not say that Schubert is at his best in these sonatas as a whole, but I have a great admiration for parts of them, especially for the last one in B flat with the exquisite andante in C sharp minor. Taking them all in all, I do not know but that I prefer his sonatas even to his short pieces for the piano. Yet they are never played at concerts!

Just as the "Impromptus" and "Musical Moments" were the source of the large crop of romantic short pieces, so Schubert's charming waltzes were the predecessors of the Lanner and Strauss dances on the one hand, and of Chopin's waltzes on the other. There is an astounding number of these Schubert dance pieces; they are charming as originally written, and Liszt has given some of them a brilliant setting for the concert hall. In this humble sphere, as in the more exalted ones we have discussed, historians have hardly given Schubert full credit for his originality and influence.

In Schubert's pianoforte music, perhaps even more than in his other compositions, we find a Slavic trait which he was the first to introduce prominently into art-music, namely, the quaint alternation of major and minor within the same period. Nor is this the only Slavic or Hungarian trait to be found in his music. During his residence in Hungary, he assimilated national melodies and rhythmic peculiarities, and embodied them in his art, thus becoming the forerunner of Liszt, Brahms, and others who have made Hungarian melodies an integral part of European concert music. From the rich stores of Slavic folk-music, in its Hungarian, Russian, Bohemian, and Polish varieties, the composers of to-day have derived, and will continue to derive, much that is charming and novel in their music. Nor is there anything objectionable in this, for if the poet and the painter base much of their best art on national legends, songs, and traditions, why should not the musician? And to Schubert will belong the honor of having been one of the first to show the way.***

IGOR STRAVINSKY

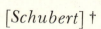

[*Schubert*] †

***Schubert is, I think, infinitely the richest of the composers you mention [Weber, Mendelssohn, Schubert, Schumann, Chopin]. As a student in St. Petersburg I knew his songs, piano music, quintets, quartets, trios,

† From Igor Stravinsky and Robert Craft, *Dialogues and a Diary*, Garden City, New York, 1963, pp. 66–67.

the last two symphonies, but little else. I was especially fond of the song cycles, though I considered that Schubert abused—was too ready to go to—the minor key, and that the strictly harmonic function of the piano and the resulting eternally arpeggiated piano accompaniments were monotonous.

Other young St. Petersburg musicians knew even less Schubert, which did not keep them from dismissing him as a "peasant musician" and, in one case, from asserting that Tchaikovsky had improved the theme of the "Unfinished" Symphony in the theme song of *Swan Lake*. Few of my fellow students listened more deeply than that, though to compare the Schubert B-minor symphony with *Swan Lake* is to learn, among many other things, that the Austrian peasant at least re-assigns orchestral roles when he repeats and that he is never as square of phrase as my compatriot.***

AARON COPLAND

[*A Schubert Melody*] †

An admirable example of pure melodic invention, which has been quoted many times, is the second theme from the first movement of Schubert's *"Unfinished" Symphony*. The "rules" of melodic construction will be of no help to anyone in analyzing this phrase. It has a curious way of seeming to fall back upon itself (or, more exactly, the G and the D), which is all the more noticeable because of the momentary reaching for a higher interval in the sixth measure. Despite its great simplicity, it makes a unique impression, reminding us of no other theme in musical literature.

† From Aaron Copland, *What to Listen for in Music*, New York, 1953, p. 36.

CHRISTA LANDON

From *New Schubert Finds* †

Together with Dr. Walther Dürr and Dr. Arnold Feil, both of Tübingen, Christa Landon of Vienna is one of the general editors of the *Neue Schubert-Ausgabe*. She and Dr. Feil edited the first musical volume of the new complete edition, Schubert's first three symphonies (Kassel, 1967), and she has edited an excellent complete edition of the Haydn piano sonatas (Vienna, 1963–66).

For many years she was one of the closest friends to Otto Erich Deutsch, whose essay *The Riddle of the Unfinished* is reprinted in this volume. Deutsch, who enriched the field of Schubert scholarship for more than sixty years, instigated the *Neue Schubert-Ausgabe* and produced for it the most recent version of his monumental documentary biography, *Schubert: Die Dokumente seines Lebens* (Kassel, 1964). As a result of her familiarity with Deutsch's personal materials—this included his heavily annotated copy of the *Schubert Thematic Catalogue* (London, 1951), which he was preparing for a German edition but never completed—Mrs. Landon discovered in the archive of the Wiener Männergesang-Verein a large group of Schubert manuscripts, copies, and arrangements. Among the manuscripts is "the earliest known autograph as well as possibly the last leaf of music that exists in Schubert's hand." Of special interest for this volume, the collection also includes Anselm Hüttenbrenner's arrangement for piano duet of the B Minor Symphony, and most important of all, an additional page, in Schubert's own hand, of the orchestral score for the Scherzo.

The newly found Schubertiana, listed here in the form of an inventory, include three different categories, each of which is important for Schubert research. Naturally the unknown autographs from all periods of his creative life are the most fascinating and most important part of these finds. Apart from the six minuets they are mainly of interest to the student: early attempts at composition, drafts, sketches, fragments and studies. The often repeated assumption that Schubert composed like a

† From Christa Landon, *New Schubert Finds*, in *The Music Review*, XXXI/3 (August 1970), 230, 225–26. Reprinted by permission of the author and *The Music Review*. Originally appeared (in German) in *Österrichische Musikzeitschrift*, XXIV/5–6 (May–June 1969), 299–323.

"sleep walker" without sufficient theoretical knowledge, has already been disproved in Alfred Orel's *Der junge Schubert (Aus der Lernzeit des Künstlers)*. The Deutsch Catalogue lists other composition exercises which are still unpublished. Fritz Racek, in his essay *Von den Schubert-Handschriften der Stadtbibliothek*,[1] mentions a number of unknown fugue exercises. The newly found studies, particularly the three long fugues, illustrate once again Schubert's preoccupation with the tools of his trade, necessary even for a genius.

* * *

MS. T

D 759, Symphony in B minor, the *Unfinished*, third movement, *Allegro*, bars 10–20, score. The following parts are filled in: first and second violins, viola, flutes, oboes, bassoons and clarinets [see above, pp. 68–69]. 1 leaf (*verso* blank), 16-stave paper, oblong folio.

So far of the third movement only the first page has been known in score (bars 1–9). These nine bars, orchestrated by Schubert, have repeatedly been published, usually together with the existing two-stave drafts for this movement.[2] These drafts include the Scherzo and the first part of the Trio. The score of the first nine bars was first printed in the *Revisionsbericht* to the old Complete Edition (1897) with the following remark: *"Weiter kam Schubert nicht; die darauffolgende Seite in der Partitur ist leer."* ("Schubert got no farther; the following page of the score is blank.") In checking the autograph, however, it became evident that the leaf which originally followed after this page, had been cut out. The detached leaf has now been found. It is leaf 2 of the fifth sheet of a gathering of six, and its edge fits exactly with that of the corresponding leaf 1 to form one sheet. The four remaining leaves are blank and make up the rest of the gathering.

It is probable that Schubert himself removed the leaf from the manuscript. The beginning of the Scherzo remained because it was written on the back of the last page of the second movement.

In the spring of 1865 Johann Herbeck brought the autograph to Vienna and, on 17th December, 1865, performed the two completed

---

1. Cf. *Festschrift zum hundertjährigen Bestehen der Wiener Stadtbibliothek, 1856–1956*, pp. 98–124.

2. A facsimile of this page in score was first published by L. Herbeck in *Johann Herbeck . . .* , after p. 168. Cf. also the facsimile edition of the autograph of the *Unfinished* in the possession of the Gesellschaft der Musikfreunde, Vienna (Drei-Masken-Verlag, München, 1923).

movements for the first time in a concert of the Gesellschaft der Musikfreunde. Until then the manuscript had been with Anselm Hüttenbrenner in Styria. The drafts for this symphony were not found until the eighties.

The hitherto unknown leaf of the score—now really the last—appears to have been kept by Schubert, and to have remained with his family after his death. It came later into the possession of the Wiener Männergesang-Verein, together with the other newly found autographs. After more than 145 years as a Sleeping Beauty, it has now reached the light of the day, making no other claim than that of being the last page in score of this famous work.[3]

3. Herbeck certainly knew nothing of this leaf, nor of the other newly discovered autographs. *Cf.*, for instance, Sir George Grove's commonplace book, MS. 2134, in the Royal College of Music, London. Grove and Arthur Sullivan travelled to Vienna in October, 1867, in search of Schubertiana. The entry relating to the autograph of the B minor Symphony reads: *"Schubert's B-minor Symphony./The following is the beginning of the Scherzo, of which 9 bars only exist./This was shown us by Herbeck . . .".* Then follows a short score of the first nine bars.

LUKAS FOSS

~⚬~

[*Beethoven and Schubert: A Comment*] †

***a composer is not always aware when he has made something of someone else's his own, which is the way all composers have generally worked. Schubert set out to write in the Beethoven style and ended up writing himself.

† From an interview with Lukas Foss (b. 1922), American composer, conductor and pianist, dated July 13, 1949. Quoted in Julia Smith, *Aaron Copland: His Work and Contribution to American Music*, New York, 1955, p. 288.

Bibliography

GENERAL

Abraham, Gerald (ed.), *The Music of Schubert,* New York, 1947.

Brown, Maurice J. E. *Essays on Schubert,* New York, 1966.

Brown, Maurice J. E., *Schubert: A Critical Biography,* London, 1958.

Deutsch, Otto E., *Schubert: Memoirs by his Friends,* New York, 1958. (Abbreviated here as *S:MF.*)

Deutsch, Otto E., *The Schubert Reader,* New York, 1947. (Abbreviated here as *SR.*)

Deutsch, Otto E. and Donald R. Wakeling, *Schubert: Thematic Catalogue,* London, 1951. (Abbreviated as *D.*)

Einstein, Alfred, *Schubert: A Musical Portrait,* New York, 1951.

Georgiades, Thrasybulos G., *Schubert: Musik und Lyrik,* Göttingen, 1967.

Kreissle von Hellborn, Heinrich, *The Life of Franz Schubert,* 2 vols., transl. by A. D. Coleridge and with an appendix on the symphonies by George Grove, London, 1869.

INDIVIDUAL STUDIES

Carner, Mosco, *The Orchestral Music,* in Gerald Abraham (ed.), *The Music of Schubert,* New York, 1947, pp. 17–87.

Carse, Adam, *Editing Schubert's Unfinished Symphony,* in *Musical Times,* XCV (1954), 143–45.

Chusid, Martin, *Schubert's Cyclic Compositions of 1824,* in *Acta Musicologica,* XXXVI (1964), 37–45.

Chusid, Martin, *Schubert's Overture for String Quintet and Cherubini's Overture to Faniska,* in *Journal of the American Musicological Society,* XV (1962), 78–84.

Frimmel, Theodor, *Beethoven und Schubert,* in *Die Musik,* XVII (1925), 401–16.

Koeltzsch, Hans, *Franz Schuberts Klaviersonaten,* Leipzig, 1927.

Kunze, Stefan, *Franz Schubert: Sinfonie h-moll, Unvollendete (Meisterwerke der Musik,* Heft I), Munich, 1965.

Laaff, Ernst, *Franz Schuberts Sinfonien,* Wiesbaden, 1933.

Laaff, Ernst, *Schuberts h-moll Symphonie,* in *Gedenkschrift für H. Abert,* Halle, 1928, pp. 93–115.

Peyser, Herbert F., *The Epic of the 'Unfinished,'* in *The Musical Quarterly*, XIV (1928), 639–60.

Pritchard, T. C. L., *The Unfinished Symphony*, in *The Music Review*, III (1942), 10–32.

Salzer, Felix, *Die Sonatenform bei Schubert*, in *Studien zur Musikwissenschaft*, XV (1928).

Tovey, Donald F., *Tonality in Schubert*, in *The Main Stream of Music and Other Essays*, New York, 1959, pp. 134–59.

Therstappen, Hans J., *Die Entwicklung der Form bei Schubert: dargestellt an den ersten Sätzen seiner Sinfonien*, Kiel, 1931.

Truscott, Harold, *Schubert's B Minor Symphony*, in *The Music Review*, XXIII (1962), 1–6.

———, *Franz Schubert*, in Robert Simpson (ed.), *The Symphony*, Baltimore, Md., 1966, I, 188–208.